# Foundations of Music

*A Computer-Assisted Introduction*

**4th Edition**

Robert Nelson
*Moores School of Music*
*University of Houston*

Carl J. Christensen
*Hartnell College*

## Wadsworth
Thomson Learning™

Australia • Canada • Denmark • Japan • Mexico • New Zealand • Philippines
Puerto Rico • Singapore • South Africa • Spain • United Kingdom • United States

Editor: Clark Baxter
Assistant Editor: Cherie Hackelberg
Editorial Assistant: Melissa Gleason
Senior Development Editor: Sharon Adams Poore
Project Editor: John Walker
Production: Greg Hubit Bookworks
Print Buyer: Stacey Weinberger

Permissions Editor: Susan Walters
Copy Editor: Margaret Moore
Designer: Ellen Pettengell Design
Autographer: Mansfield Music-Graphics
Cover Designer: Ark Stein/The Visual Group
Compositor: Susan Rogin Type+Design
Printer: Malloy Lithographing, Inc.

Printed in the United States of America

2  3  4  5  6  03  02  01  00

For permission to use material from this text,
contact us by
  **Web:** www.thomsonrights.com
  **Fax:** 1-800-730-2215
  **Phone:** 1-800-730-2214

For more information, contact
**Wadsworth/Thomson Learning**
**10 Davis Drive**
**Belmont, CA 94002-3098**
**USA**
**www.wadsworth.com**

**International Headquarters**
Thomson Learning
290 Harbor Drive, 2nd Floor
Stamford, CT 06902-7477
USA

**UK/Europe/Middle East**
Thomson Learning
Berkshire House
168-173 High Holborn
London WC1V 7AA
United Kingdom

**Asia**
Thomson Learning
60 Albert Street #15-01
Albert Complex
Singapore 189969

**Canada**
Nelson/Thomson Learning
1120 Birchmount Road
Scarborough, Ontario M1K 5G4
Canada

**Library of Congress Cataloging-in-Publication Data**
Nelson, Robert.
    Foundations of music: a computer-assisted introduction/
Robert Nelson, Carl J. Christensen. — 4th ed.
    p.  cm.
    Includes index.
    ISBN 0-534-56764-9
    1. Music—Theory—Computer-assisted instruction.
    I. Christensen, Carl J.   II. Title.
MT6.N225F7   2000
781'.076—dc21                                  99-27833

 This book is printed on acid-free recycled paper.

# Contents

# Preface

## "I WANT TO LEARN ABOUT MUSIC!"

This is a fair enough request and one commonly heard on college campuses. The student may be motivated by nothing more than the desire to fulfill a fine arts requirement in a painless way, but our experience has taught us that the student is just as likely to have some prior experience with music—playing in a "garage" band, taking a few piano lessons long ago—or just enjoys listening to music and genuinely wants to know more about it. In each case, the student hopes that a course or two in music will increase his or her understanding and thereby enhance and deepen his or her musical experiences. Unless such students elect to major in music, in all likelihood their choice will be either a music "appreciation" course or a course in music fundamentals. This may be supplemented with beginning study in piano or some other instrument. This book is intended for use in music fundamentals classes for non–music majors at the college level, but it could also be used successfully at the advanced high school level or as a supplement to first-year theory for college-level music majors. It should also integrate nicely with any methods for beginning instruments.

Realistically, the number of hours that nonmajors can devote to fine arts is limited. Given this fact, any fine arts course—broadly defined—should provide some overview of the subject matter, impart useful facts or skills, and ultimately provide the critical bases for a greater understanding that one hopes will lead to greater enjoyment and broadened tastes.

## "THIS IS A MAJOR SCALE. SO WHAT?"

Those of us in music have, at some time, endured a great deal of drudgery in learning our scales and key signatures. We take it for granted that this is important. But students at the college level will be coming from a much different frame of reference.

- They may know nothing about music—only that you listen to it.
- They may play by ear but are unable to express verbally what they are doing, much less write it down. Yet they may really be quite musically intuitive.
- They may have a smattering of knowledge of scales and key signatures and very likely knowledge of a few chords.

What they all want (and need) is to be able to deal with notated music as they encounter it in sheet music, songbooks, hymnals, or their elementary piano music.

It seems to us that too many rudiments books present only the raw material of music without going that one step further and presenting a clear and simple context within which the student can see the operation, and in fact the very rationale, for the materials being studied.

Our attempt is to present rudiments holistically—by always relating the fundamentals being studied to actual musical practice through copious musical examples. These examples have been carefully graded for comprehension, and questions for guided discussion have been included throughout. This approach has proven successful at more advanced levels, and we feel that it stimulates the learning process.

We have chosen musical examples from a wide variety of historical periods and genres, including popular music. The intent has been to move from examples that are familiar to those less well known.

## "THAT SOUNDS NICE. WHAT IS IT?"

Musical literacy involves two complementary skills—reading and writing —and exercises for both are found throughout the book. But above all, perhaps, music involves listening skills. One applies "book knowledge" to an aural experience, and in that aspect music is unlike any other art form. Consequently, the importance of looking and listening to actual music from the outset cannot be overstated. Suggested Listening assignments have been included where new topics are introduced. In many respects, students can *hear* concepts prior to their being able to *read* and understand them. And it is always worthwhile to relate the aural experience to the actual study of the musical concept at hand. The listening examples should, of course, be discussed. As with the printed examples, the goal has been breadth of style and idiom. Many of the Suggested Listening examples and other musical illustrations will be found on the accompanying CD-ROM. These recorded examples may be played through the computer or on a regular CD player. Where it was not possible to provide the recorded examples, discographies have been included. References to readily available recordings appear just below the particular musical example.

## "AT LAST! MY OWN (DIGITAL) TUTOR!"

There's no escaping the fact that fluency in music requires a sure and thorough acquaintance with key signatures, the various forms of scales, intervals, and the like. Music teachers know from long experience that these topics can really be absorbed only by drill and repetition—the same techniques so indispensable to learning basic arithmetic or spelling.

Up to now, this has meant both a large investment in class time—leaving less time for more musical pursuits—and a necessary redundancy in the amount and types of writing and recognition drills. We feel that "programmed" texts have been largely unsatisfactory. First, the student must use the frames "honestly"—that is, he or she must do all of them, in order, and not peek. Second, the frames never change, in effect limiting the amount of variety and redundancy in the problems. Third, and most important, "programmed" texts cannot by their very nature deal with the intangibles one finds in even the simplest piece of music.

Our book deals with the problem by incorporating computer-assisted exercises. The advantages of using the computer are manifold:

- Drill and practice are made more enjoyable. Almost all students report that the interactive audio-visual aspect of the computer makes learning more fun.
- The interactive nature of the exercises helps the student learn as a participant rather than as a mere observer. There is very little flashcard-style drill. Rather, the student is asked to add measure lines, complete measures, add accidentals, or spell chords. For every topic, there are a variety of computer drills for both reading and writing

skills. This keeps the student interested and ensures the number of repetitions necessary for comprehension of the material.

- Study can be truly self-paced. Since each computer exercise drills a specific topic with a small number of problems presented repeatedly but in a random order, a student may do as few or as many repetitions as necessary. The student should work with a problem until he or she feels confident and then move on to the next problem or level. If the student encounters difficulties with the written exercises in the book, he or she should return to the computer for additional drill. The computer exercises are also an excellent source for later review. *Since all the material is cumulative, the student cannot make real progress unless each step along the way is thoroughly mastered.* Experience has shown us that the computer is an invaluable tool for achieving this mastery, but only if it is used!
- The computer provides instant correction. The student does not have to wait several days for homework to be returned to find out if the work was done correctly.
- The computer can actually play the music notated on the screen. Scale and chord-spelling exercises take on a whole new relevance when the student can listen to the effect of accidentals as they are added.
- Every drill gives the student the opportunity to hear what he or she has written. The computer even allows the student to hear and compare right and wrong responses. In addition, the instruction pages for many of the drills give demonstrations of the materials in question, such as scales or triads.
- Since it is so important for the student to have a sense of how the music sounds, the CD-ROM accompanying the book contains a folder of MIDI files as well as numerous recorded examples. The MIDI files can be accessed by your computer's multimedia software or a MIDI sequencer program. The MIDI files provide interactive demonstrations of particular sound and rhythmic concepts. The recorded examples can be played either on the computer or on a regular CD player. This feature gives the student the opportunity to listen to and study many of the musical illustrations contained in the book.
- All the programs can be used on a standard computer. There is no need to buy expensive add-ons.
- Finally, all of this individual drill happens in a private, uncritical environment. The computer is a tireless tutor with infinite patience!

At the same time, we feel that the computer, though a versatile and useful tool, cannot replace the instructor in the classroom. This is particularly true when dealing with the subtleties of the actual music. For best results, the instructor should present the material in class, utilizing as completely as possible the Suggested Listening examples and the musical examples printed in the book. The latter should be sung or played in class. Chord symbols are in many cases supplied so that guitar or autoharp can be used—along with piano—for accompaniment.

Wherever the symbol for the computer-assisted instruction appears, the student should go to the computer and drill on the given materials. The computer-assisted instruction is designed for individual pacing, instant grading, and correction as needed; it can also provide a log of exercises attempted and the cumulative score. The computer drills are user friendly, in that no prior experience with a computer is required. The instructor may want to begin with a group session with the computer to allay the fears of those students not so technologically inclined.

Written exercises may be assigned at the instructor's discretion. These exercises develop writing skills and are intended to complement the work on the computer.

Additional written exercises can be produced at any time by simply printing out a page from any of the computer drills. The computer will randomly select a number of problems and format a page that can be handed in for grading.

## "THE FOCUS IS ALWAYS ON THE MUSIC."

Class time saved should be devoted to a listening to and discussion of Music for Study sections. Every attempt has been made to supply a breadth of style and idioms, but the instructor may wish to have students bring in their own examples—particularly pop music.

A word about sequence: Most of the materials presented in this book build in a logical progression from simple to more complex concepts. It is assumed that students will master one skill before going on to others. In most cases the instructor will be comfortable following the book's sequence. There shouldn't be great difficulties, however, should one wish to change the order. The students in a music rudiments course will most likely demonstrate a widely diverse range of backgrounds and experience with music. Given this circumstance, the instructor may find that there is more material in this book than can reasonably be covered in one semester. Since this book is often used in review courses for music majors, it seemed best to be comprehensive.

The most basic and essential topics are covered in the first twelve chapters. Classes that are interested (and adequately prepared) will find additional materials in Chapter 13, "Topics for Enrichment and Further Study." Here the student will find information on other scales and meters, along with a discussion of their relevance to other styles and musical cultures; additional chord types commonly found in both classical and popular music; and additional creative exercises. There are also computer drills that will help in the exploration of most of these topics. Yet while interesting, these topics are not critical to the understanding of the fundamental skills required for reading and writing music, and instructors should not be concerned if the limited time of a one-semester course prevents their inclusion. If there is the luxury of a second semester of rudiments, the instructor—after the necessary period of review—may wish to begin with Chapter 13 and then go back and pursue such topics as form in greater detail.

In this regard, a few cautionary notes. While we have tried to be both complete and comprehensive, there is always the necessary limitation of space. Instructors are encouraged to expand on our presentation with additional explanation and examples drawn from their own rich musical experience. The amount of space in the book devoted to a given topic is not always a reliable guide to the amount of time that it will take for that topic to be confidently understood. Compound meter, for example, is typically more difficult than simple meter, and intervals, which can be presented in a misleadingly succinct manner, traditionally require a great amount of time and a number of repetitions to be grasped securely.

And finally, music is never as crystal clear as we might like. There will always be a few ambiguities. Encourage the students to ask questions. At some point, the complete answer to their questions might be found in further study in music theory. Remember, as an instructor you will be opening doors. Give them a sure footing in the basics, and then wish them a *bon voyage* as they go on exploring the many worlds of music.

We would like to acknowledge the following people for their aid and encouragement in the preparation of this book:

- Joy Nelson, California State University, Fresno; Herbert Bielawa, San Francisco State University; Robert Placek, University of Georgia; and Alan E. Stanek, Idaho State University, for their assistance in reviewing the first-edition manuscript.
- Mark Boling (software review), University of Tennessee; William A. Hawkins, Palomar Community College; Robert Maddalena, Merced

College; Claire McCoy, University of Minnesota; Ronald J. Sherrod, Grossmont College; Alan E. Stanek, Idaho State University; and Frances Ulrich, California State University, Northridge, for their reviews of the second edition.

- Nancy Bachmann (software), Los Medanos College; Scott Bowen, San Joaquin Delta College; Scott Henderson, Cerritos College; Charles Jennings (software), San Joaquin Delta College; John Maltester, Los Medanos College; Ron Matthews, Eastern College; and George Weimer, University of Indianapolis, for their reviews of the third edition.

- Eugene H. Bullock-Wilson (software review); Patricia B. Helm, Colby College; Nathan J. Kreitzer, Santa Barbara City College; Julie M. Maisel, Millsaps College; Barbara Powell, Delta College; and David Kenneth Smith, University of Alabama, Huntsville, for their reviews of the fourth edition.

- Michael Greene for invaluable assistance with Windows™ programming.

- Reynaldo Ochoa for recording and editing the many musical examples. Thanks also to Justin White and Ruth Tomfohrde, faculty members at the Moores School of Music, for performing the vocal examples, and to John Proffitt, the general manager of KUHF radio, for his invaluable assistance in tracking down recordings of the orchestral examples. All the recordings were made in the Goldmark Recording Studio at the Moores School of Music.

- Our many students who helped test our materials and offered many helpful suggestions.

- Carl Mann for proofing the typescript and to the indefatigable Margaux Mann for her countless hours slaving over a hot word processor.

- Lastly, a special thanks to Carole and JoAnn for supporting us in so many ways during the development of this book.

# Use of the Computer

## "USE IT!"

The CD-ROM accompanying this book contains exercises that provide an effective and enjoyable means to quickly master the material presented in the text. Instructors are encouraged to do the following:

- **Consider the computer exercises homework.** Instructors are urged to use the "Computer-Assisted Instruction: Contents and Log" section of the text to assign specific numbers of repetitions of specific exercise levels and to request a printed copy of student RECORDS from each student. The process of producing this printout is explained below. Notice that each level has a unique number for this purpose, from #1 to #159.
- **Be selective.** The disk contains a massive amount of material. Instructors should assign specific exercises and make it clear which topics need not be drilled; for example, alto clef probably would be omitted in an entry-level general education class.
- **Use the worksheets.** Each exercise offers an opportunity to print out a worksheet on Postscript printers, only. These randomly generated sheets (they will all be different) may be used as quizzes or extra homework. Print them at 80–90% reduction for a more professional appearance.

The following points will be helpful to students:

- **Use the computer!** Each computer exercise drills a specific topic. As soon as a given topic is covered in class and the indication for computer-assisted instruction ⌨ appears in the text, go to the computer and do a significant number of the indicated exercises.

- **Do a significant number of repetitions.** In most cases, you should do at least twenty repetitions in each section of each assigned exercise. There are very few flashcard-style drills. Rather, you will be asked to add measure lines, complete measures, build scales, or spell chords. Both reading and writing skills are developed. Concepts that are explained in a few short paragraphs in the text may require an extended session with the computer to really master.

- **Help!** While doing the exercises, you may select a Help option. This will return you to the instructions for help with the mechanics of the exercise. Many of the instruction screens also provide on-screen explanation of the material and will also play the scale or chord while the sounding notes are highlighted in red.

- **Don't be afraid to make mistakes!** In almost all of the exercises, you will be given several chances to modify your answer. In any case, the computer will eventually satisfy your curiosity by providing the correct answer and the same problem will eventually reappear. Also, upon leaving each exercise you will be given the option of NOT saving your scores during that session.

## EXPLORE MUSIC WITH THE COMPUTER

- **Recorded examples.** Be sure to explore the actual sound of pieces of music discussed in the text. Many of the Suggested Listening examples and other musical illustrations are recorded on the CD-ROM. They can be played on the computer or on an ordinary CD player. Look for the CD icon ◉ .

- **Demonstrations.** As mentioned above, many of the instruction screens for the *Foundations of Music* computer program contain demonstrations of the material. Scale and chords will play with each note being highlighted in red as it plays. The *Other Scales Demonstration* module plays the scales as well as melodies that are also printed in the text.

- **MIDI files.** The CD-ROM also contains a folder of standard MIDI files. Using your computer's multimedia software or a MIDI sequencer program, you can listen to these pieces. Some of the files demonstrate articulations from Chapter 1 and others demonstrate various meters. All the music of these MIDI sequences is printed in the text. Experiment playing the files with different timbres.

- **Have fun!** Three of the exercises in the computer program give you a chance to compose music: Rhythmic Composition—Simple Meters (#46), Rhythmic Composition—Compound Meters (#85), and Melodic Composition (#154). Notate your music on the screen, have the computer play it, change any note you want, and then print it out. Enjoy!

# USING THE CD-ROM

- **Contents of the CD-ROM.** The CD-ROM disk accompanying the book contains both the Macintosh and Windows versions of the computer program. Everything for the Macintosh user is inside a folder titled MAC and everything for the Windows user is in a folder titled WINDOWS. The disk also contains audio tracks that can be played on the computer or on an ordinary CD player. Within the MAC and WINDOWS folders are folders containing MIDI files for that platform.
- **Using the CD-ROM.** The program needs to be installed on the hard disk of a computer, and the student's scores or records are stored on any hard or floppy drive connected to the computer. Students who will always use the same computer may save their scores on its hard drive. Students who store their records on a floppy may use any computer or network that has the program installed.
- **Fonts.** The program uses its own font for displaying musical symbols. This font is attached as a resource to the Macintosh program, but it must be installed in the Windows environment (see below).
- **Student records.** The record of the total problems attempted for each drill and the number of correct responses is stored in a file that is named by the student the first time the student uses the program. During subsequent sessions the student should open this file from the FILE menu on the main title screen and continue working. The files are encrypted and can be read only from within the *Foundations* program. In other words, students could place their records files in a given folder on a network and the instructor could review them using RECORDS from the FILE menu of the main title screen of the *Foundations* program.

# FIRST USE—
# MACINTOSH USERS, ONLY

This disk may be used on any Macintosh computer (System 7.5.3 or higher) with a CD-ROM drive. The disk is not copy-protected and may be copied to a hard drive or server.

- **Installing the program.** Turn on the computer; wait until the "desktop" appears; insert the *Foundations* disk into the CD-ROM drive. Open the MAC folder on the CD-ROM. Locate the *Foundations of Music* icon. At this point the program may be copied to the computer's hard drive or it may be run from the CD-ROM. If you wish to run it off the hard drive, drag the icon to the hard-drive icon.
- **Starting the program.** Start the program by double-clicking on the *Foundations of Music* icon. When the main title screen appears, pull down the FILE menu and select "Register a New Student." Follow the instructions to enter your name and to save the file containing your name and scores. This file will obviously have to be saved on the computer's hard drive or on a floppy disk.

# FIRST USE—
# WINDOWS USERS, ONLY

This CD-ROM requires Windows 95 or higher. The program must be installed on a hard drive or server.

- **Installing the program.** Start the computer, then insert the *Foundations* CD-ROM in the CD-ROM drive. Use "My Computer" to locate the CD-ROM. Open the WINDOWS folder and double-click on the SETUP icon. Install the program in any directory on Drive C or other hard drive on the network.
- **Installing the "Music2" font.** From the START menu select SETTINGS, then CONTROL PANEL, then FONTS. From the FILE menu of the FONTS control panel, select INSTALL NEW FONT. Locate the font "Music2" on the *Foundations* CD-ROM and install it.
- **Starting the program.** The installation program should have placed the *Foundations of Music* program in the list of programs on the START menu. The program can also be started by locating its icon on the hard drive using "My Computer" and double-clicking on the

icon. When the main title screen appears, pull down the FILE menu and select "Register a New Student." Follow the instructions to enter your name and to save the file containing your name and scores. This file will obviously have to be saved on the computer's hard drive or on a floppy disk.

## SUBSEQUENT USES

- **Using the program after it has been installed.** In Windows, run the *Foundations* program from the START menu or locate the icon using "My Computer" and double-click on the icon. On the Mac, locate the *Foundations* icon and double-click on the icon.
- **Loading your records.** When the main title screen appears, pull down the FILE menu and select "Open File for an Existing Student." Use the controls in the dialog box to locate your previously saved file, open it, and continue working.

## MACINTOSH AND WINDOWS USERS

Each version of the software contains exactly the same exercises with exactly the same 159 specific drills. Some students in a given class may use the Mac version while others use the Windows version. Both versions will print out student records and worksheets.

- **Finding the exercises.** The thirteen pull-down menus at the top of the main title screen correspond to the thirteen chapters of the text. Place the pointer on Chapter 1 and hold the mouse button down. While still holding the button down, drag the mouse straight down and notice that exercise names are highlighted. To select an exercise, release the mouse button as the name of the exercise is highlighted.

    Once you are in an exercise, the name of the exercise will appear at the top of the screen. Select a specific drill by using the pull-down menu. Notice that each indication for computer-assisted instruction in the text guides you to a given chapter and topic, and then asks you to do a specific drill. Follow this path by making the appropriate selection from each pull-down menu as it appears. In actually doing the exercises, you will respond in most cases by placing the pointer on the correct response or location and clicking the mouse button.

When you finish a drill, you may return to the title screen by selecting QUIT.

- **Saving your records.** At the end of each drill, you are given the option of saving the scores from that session. If you select this option, the total number of problems that you attempted and total number of correct responses will be added to those of previous sessions and stored in your records file.
- **Printing student records.** From the main title screen, you may view the record of your progress by selecting RECORDS from the FILE pull-down menu. This selection also offers the option of printing a copy of your records to turn in to your instructor as evidence of your independent study.
- **To end.** To end a study session, select QUIT from the main title screen FILE menu and you will be returned to the desktop.
- **Subsequent sessions.** Remember that during subsequent sessions you will use the "Open File for an Existing Student" option from the FILE menu of the main title screen to begin your session.

# Computer-Assisted Instruction: Contents and Log

Use this log to note the exercises assigned by your instructor. The indications in the column on the right may be used to identify specific levels of an exercise. You may want to record the number of problems that you have done on each exercise. This information will also be recorded on the disk as you finish each exercise.

## Pitch Notation

1. Pitch Naming
   Treble Clef
   
   No Ledger Lines ............................... #10 _____

   Using Ledger Lines ........................... #11 _____

   Bass Clef

   No Ledger Lines ............................... #12 _____

   Using Ledger Lines ........................... #13 _____

   Grand Staff

   No Ledger Lines ............................... #14 _____

   Using Ledger Lines ........................... #15 _____

   Tenor Clef

   No Ledger Lines ............................... #16 _____

   Using Ledger Lines ........................... #17 _____

   Alto Clef

   No Ledger Lines ............................... #18 _____

   Using Ledger Lines ........................... #19 _____

2. Pitch Writing
   Treble Clef ...................................... #20 _____

   Bass Clef ........................................ #21 _____

   Grand Staff ...................................... #22 _____

   Tenor Clef ...................................... #23 _____

   Alto Clef ........................................ #24 _____

3. Piano Keyboard ................................ #25 _____

# CHAPTER 3: SIMPLE METER

1. Inserting Barlines—Simple Meters

   $\frac{4}{4}$  $\frac{3}{4}$  $\frac{2}{4}$  .......... #26 _____

   $\frac{4}{2}$  $\frac{3}{2}$  $\frac{2}{2}$  .......... #27 _____

   $\frac{4}{8}$  $\frac{3}{8}$  $\frac{2}{8}$  .......... #28 _____

   All of the Above ............................... #29 _____

# CHAPTER 4: SCALES

## Whole Steps and Half Steps

# CHAPTER 6: THE MINOR MODE

## Minor Scale Forms

# CHAPTER 9: INTERVALS

# CHAPTER 10: CHORDS AND HARMONY

# Introduction

## Suggested Listening

*Listen to short examples from a wide variety of sources. Include classical music from several periods, popular music, show tunes, even folk music and music from other cultures, if desired. The class may wish to submit examples from their own collections. In discussion, consider the following:*

1. What do all the examples have in common? What common properties are in evidence?
2. What differentiates the examples? What gives each piece its unique characteristics? Is the music simple or complex? How many performers seem to be involved?
3. How does the music affect your emotions or feelings? To what general musical characteristics might you be reacting?

*Don't be concerned with using any musical terms for the time being. Rather, describe your sensations very generally.*

In times past, a cultivated person was expected to have some firsthand familiarity with one of the fine arts, whether painting, music, drama, or literature. And while some aspired to be what in our day would be called professionals, many others avidly became amateurs—in the original meaning of "lovers of the arts," rather than in the sometimes demeaning or pejorative sense. They wanted to be active rather than passive participants in music making.

Today we are more than likely "consumers" of the arts—audience rather than participant. While we still value the concept of cultural "refinement," we must often be content with a few "appreciation" courses in college or season's tickets to the symphony or theater. And though we wouldn't deny that even passive involvement in the arts is a positive thing, many of us still regret at one time or another that we didn't stay with those piano lessons, or that we never got around to *really* learning the guitar, or that we never knew the pleasure of gathering around the parlor piano for an old-fashioned song fest.

No matter. Perhaps it's never too late—at least to enjoy music first-hand, whether as a player or a singer or just a listener. But as with so many other endeavors, the more we know about something, the more enjoyment we derive from it. This is all the more true with music, which has its own peculiar and largely symbolic language.

What is offered in this book is the fundamentals of musical literacy. This is a primer, if you will—the grammar of the musical language. Reading this book and doing the exercises will *not* make you an instant performer or composer! But it should open doors—doors to enhanced appreciation of all the music around you, and doors that beckon to a friendlier world of actual *doing,* by unlocking the mysteries of musical notation and thus of music itself.

This book follows the traditional progression from the rudiments—note values, pitch notation, scales, and key signatures—through intervals and chord structures to a preliminary treatment of phrase structure and musical form. Throughout the book, as much music as possible has been incorporated. In the early sections, your comprehension may be minimal; but rather than being discouraged, you should measure your growth by the increase in understanding as you master each successive level.

As in many other endeavors, certain achievements come only with repetitions. Such is the case with our rudiments. To lighten this sometime chore, the drill exercises have been put on a computer disk. This allows you to spend whatever time is necessary to master each item. It also has the virtue of providing instant correction, and thus enhances the speed at which you develop true fluency.

The importance of this fluency cannot be understated. Since the material is cumulative, no new material should be attempted until each drill has been thoroughly mastered. And while reading the book is certainly necessary, *just* reading the book will not be sufficient.

Lastly, we must stress that musical literacy is, strictly speaking, not a goal in itself but a means to a greater end. One obviously doesn't sit down and "read" a piece of music as one does a short story or novel. Music is intended to be played or, of course, listened to. And while this book concentrates on reading and writing skills, it should prove a useful adjunct or complement to classes in piano, recorders, guitars, or other instruments.

At the same time, you are encouraged to sing or play as many of the musical examples as your level of skill will allow. Many of the musical illustrations have been chosen for familiarity or accessibility. A simple system of numbers or syllables might be used to reinforce the theoretical concepts with practical reading skills. Many of the melodies have been provided with chord symbols not solely for the study of harmony but for the in-class use of guitar or autoharp as well. The guiding philosophy throughout has been to progress from the familiar to the unfamiliar, from simple to more complex.

This book is but a first step in the study of music. The topics of harmony and form are far too broad and complex for adequate treatment here. It is hoped that with a sound fundamental training, you will be able to go on to more detailed and specialized study. At the very least, it is hoped that this book will both enrich your musical experience and encourage a continuing lively curiosity about all matters musical.

# Sound

As you discovered from all of those musical examples you were asked to listen to in the Introduction, there is an extraordinary variety of music. Yet there are just two basic properties common to all of it. All music consists of **sound** that occurs over a period of **time.** We must begin our discussion of music with an overview of sound, and we will investigate the property of time in Chapters 3, 5, and 8.

Sounds can be informally characterized with a few descriptive terms. Sounds are relatively high or low, loud or soft, brilliant or muted. Since sound is a physical phenomenon, the science of **acoustics** provides us with a more precise way of describing and measuring a given sound and comparing it with other sounds.

## PITCH AND TIMBRE; THE OVERTONE SERIES

To the physicist, sound is produced by vibrations transmitted through the air from a given vibrating medium to the complex receiver that is the human ear. The vibrating medium might be the string of a guitar or violin, or a column of air as in a trumpet, or a solid body as with certain percussion instruments.

These vibrations can be measured and analyzed. The number of vibrations that occur in a specific period of time gives us the **frequency.** Frequency is calculated in cycles per second, or *hertz* (abbreviated Hz). The fewer the hertz, the lower the sound. The lowest audible sound is around 16 Hz, the highest 20,000 (20K) Hz. In musical terms, frequency establishes the **pitch** of a sound. As we will see, pitches are given letter-names and are assigned **registers,** a designation for the relative highness or lowness of the pitch. The lowest note on the piano (AAA) is 27.5 Hz, and the highest (c5) is 4186 Hz.

All natural sounds actually consist of a complex of vibrations at various frequencies that are mathematically related. The lowest of this complex of **partials** is called the **fundamental** and is the primary determinant of the pitch of a sound. The strength, or **amplitude,** of the higher partials (called **overtones** or **harmonics**) determines the **timbre** (pronounced *tam*ber) of the sound. If the harmonics are related by what are called whole-number ratios, and the vibrations themselves are relatively regular, we describe the sound as **tone.** Most music consists of tones. If the vibrations are irregular, we describe the sound as **noise.** Normally we don't think of noises as being musical, but in fact quite a few very common percussion instruments produce noises rather than tones. Two good examples are the snare drum and the woodblock.

The whole series of overtones can be graphically represented by a series of pitches called the **overtone series.** Here are the first twelve members of the series on C, represented in standard pitch notation along with the ratios of vibration:

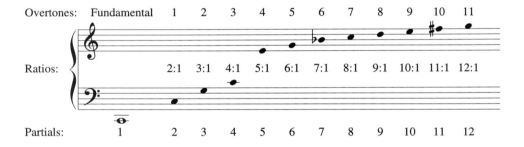

The first overtone (second partial) is of particular importance. The ratio of vibration of this overtone to the fundamental is 2:1. This is the closest possible relationship (except for 1:1 ) and makes these two pitches sound almost identical, the only difference being one of register. These two pitches are assigned the same letter-name and form the interval of the **octave.** This term, derived from the Italian word *octava* for "eight," describes the musical distance between the two pitches, which is eight steps or degrees. The octave, as we will see, becomes the basic "framing" interval for scales.

We use the term **timbre** in describing the "color" of a sound. It is this property that allows us to distinguish among the various instruments, but it may refer more generally to the brightness or dullness or darkness of a sound. Acousticians can precisely measure and graph the overtones of any given fundamental produced by any instrument.

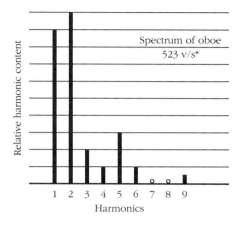

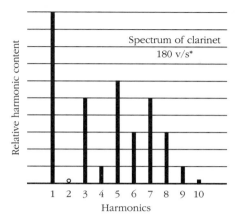

## DYNAMICS

The loudness or softness of a sound is a product of many factors. Most modern instruments can produce sounds ranging from the nearly inaudible to ear-splitting intensity, and they can vary their volume in a very controlled manner over a given period of time. Beyond this, we understand intuitively that the overall volume of sound is affected by the number of performers and the types of instruments they are playing. We expect a brass band to sound louder than a string quartet.

Those familiar with contemporary popular music will also be familiar with electro-acoustical amplification. Note that the root of the word *amplifier* is also the root of the term *amplitude*. All instruments have some kind of built-in acoustical amplifier. It may be the sounding board of the piano, or the chest of the guitar or the violin. It is this amplifier, or **resonator,** that allows us to hear the instrument from some distance. The electric amplifier takes this process one step further by translating the vibrations of the instrument into electrical current. The amplitude of the resulting electric vibrations can be significantly increased and used to drive a loud speaker, thus allowing the sound to be heard at greater volume levels or over a greater distance.

*v/s = cycles per second or rate of vibration.

It is interesting to compare the relative volumes of environmental sounds with various musical sounds. In the graph below, the relative volume levels are given in decibels, the standard scientific unit for sound levels.

The volume of sound is also affected by what we call the **texture** of the music. A given selection of music might consist of just a number of single pitches in succession—in other words, what we call a **melody** or a melodic line. Or it might consist of several strands of melody being performed simultaneously. Textures such as this are called **polyphonic** or **contrapuntal.** The technique of combining melodic lines is called **counterpoint.** Or a selection of music might consist of blocks of sound—a number of pitches occurring simultaneously. The number of pitches can vary widely from two or three up to twenty or more. We can describe these blocks of sound as having comparative densities, and we call these blocks of sound **harmonies** (singular: *harmony*) or **chord structures.**

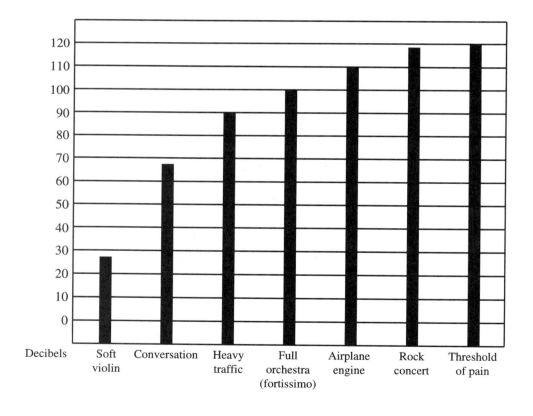

Textures that have a significant harmonic or chordal component are called **homophonic.** Included in this category is music in **chorale style,** where all the lines or voices move in the same rhythmic values, and **melody with accompaniment,** where there is one principal featured melodic line—often called the solo, implying that it would be performed by a single person—with other voices or instruments providing harmonic support—the accompaniment. We will encounter examples of each of these textures as our study progresses, and this topic will be explored in greater detail in Chapters 10 and 13.

There is the most marvelous variability among all of these factors that can be controlled by the composer or, in the case of recordings, by the sound engineer. Single notes can be played quite loudly, just as great densities of sound can be produced relatively softly.

Loudness and softness are indicated in music by **dynamic markings.** These are abbreviations of the original Italian terms:

***p*** is short for piano and means *soft.*
***f*** is short for forte and means *loud.*
***m*** is short for *mezzo* and is a qualifier meaning moderately. In combination, ***mp*** means somewhat soft and ***mf*** means somewhat loud.
***pp*** stands for *pianissimo* and means very soft.
***ff*** stands for *fortissimo* and means very loud.
Other degrees can be indicated by stringing out additional ***p***'s and ***f***'s: ***ppp, pppp, fff,*** and so on.

Dynamic changes can be indicated two ways:

1.  or *crescendo* (*cresc.*) means to increase the volume.
2.  or *diminuendo* (*dim.*) means to decrease the volume.

## Computer Exercises

Wherever the computer icon appears, you should go to the computer and drill on the exercises listed.

## Computer Exercise

Chapter 12   Looking at Music
1. Musical Terms—Dynamic Indications   Drill #155

# THE ENVELOPE; ARTICULATIONS

Some of you may have had experience working with synthesizers and will be familiar with the concept of the envelope of a sound. In simple terms, there are at least three stages in the production of a sound: the *attack,* the *steady-state period,* and the *decay,* or release, of a sound. **Attack** refers to the manner in which a sound is initiated. The beginning of a sound may be barely perceptible, or it may begin with a violent burst of air or a strong hammering motion by the bow of a violinist or by the hand of a pianist, or with any degree in between. Acoustical studies have shown that the attack transients, or complex noises produced at the initiation of a sound, are very important in allowing us to determine which instrument we are hearing. **Decay** refers to the way in which the sound stops. Sounds may gradually die away to silence, or they may stop abruptly without any change in dynamics. They may even stop with one of the strong accents described below. During the **steady-state period** of a sound, a constant source of energy must be supplied to keep the sound going. This may be the action of a bow or the breath of the performer. It is not unusual to find small fluctuations in pitch during the steady-state phase, and we already have noted that the dynamic level may be changed.

There are a number of symbols that you will encounter in a piece of music that tell the performer how to attack or release the sound. These markings fall under the broad category of **articulations.**

1. **Slurs.** Notes falling within the curved line are played or sung in a very **legato** (connected) manner.

The slur should not be confused with the tie, which connects the same pitches and is used to create values of longer duration. The tie will be explained in the next chapter.

2. **Tenuto marks** (♩) imply a soft attack and a constant steady-state for the full duration of the note. A series of tenuto notes would also be played or sung in a very legato manner.

3. **Staccato dots** indicate a light, clean attack and may mean that the notes are to be slightly shortened or separated.

A dot at the end of a slur indicates a lifting or shortening of the last note.

4. Accent marks are attack intensifiers and imply a certain additional volume or intensity. The most common ones are >, Λ, Λ, and ▼.

Closely related are the symbols *sfz* and *sf,* which stand for *sforzando,* and are used to indicate a strong accent. Accent marks generally imply separation, or *non-legato.*

# Music for Study

*Listen to the following examples as you look at the music. Interpret the dynamic and articulation marks in each. Can you hear the differences in articulations?*

**EXAMPLE 1**

*"Hunting Song"*   ROBERT SCHUMANN (1810–1856)

**EXAMPLE 2**

*"The Washington Post March (Trio)"*   JOHN PHILIP SOUSA (1854–1932)

**EXAMPLE 3**

*"Egmont Overture" (mm.\* 1–15)*   LUDWIG VAN BEETHOVEN (1770–1827)

*Music for orchestra is conventionally written in a full score where each instrument is given its own staff. This often results in a score containing 20 to 30 staves. (Staves and staff systems will be fully explained in the next chapter.) In order to make the music easier to read, orchestral music is often printed in a reduction, which is what appears below. This music can then be easily played at the piano.*

*Listen to the recording of the orchestral performance as you look at the music. Beethoven has created differences in volume or loudness by using several of the devices discussed earlier in the chapter. As you listen, interpret all the given dynamic markings. Are the differences readily apparent? There are also examples of both homophonic and polyphonic textures. The passage beginning in measure 2 and ending at the beginning of measure 5 is* **homophonic** *and is scored for the entire string section of the orchestra. Compare the sound of that passage with the sound of measures 5–8, which is* **polyphonic.** *You will clearly hear the individual lines that are initially scored for single woodwind instruments. Note the musical similarity of each line. You should also clearly hear the difference in the dynamics of this section, which not only is texturally contrasting but also is marked to be played softly.* Tutti *is an Italian term that means "all." Here it designates that the notes marked tutti will be played by the entire orchestra. You will hear the very obvious difference in volume between the tutti notes and the immediately following music, which is still* **forte** *but is played by fewer instruments.*

\*mm. is an abbreviation for measures. (m. = measure.)

*Example 3 continued*

## Computer Exercise

Chapter 1    Sound
  1. Sound Demonstration    Drill #1

## Exploring Sound at the Computer

*You can use the MIDI files of Examples 1–3 to explore the various properties of sound. These files can be accessed by your computer's multimedia software or a MIDI sequencer program.*

*Play back the melodies of Examples 1 and 2 using a variety of single instruments. Compare the timbres. Now try using a sound made up of layers, such as the pipe organ or string ensemble. Again, compare the timbres. Do the layered sounds seem to be louder? Play back the melody with various percussion sounds. Do all have pitch? How precise is the pitch of the snare drum or woodblock compared to that of the xylophone or glockenspiel?*

*Each melody is presented twice—once with just the notes, and a second time with the dynamics and articulations added. Listen for the differences. They should be apparent regardless of which sound you selected.*

*Next, play back Example 3, using first a single timbre on each channel and then using layered samples, as before. How does the density of the sound affect your perception of loudness? MIDI channel 1 represents the strings and is intended to be played with a uniform timbre, as would be the case with the string section of the orchestra. The other MIDI channels represent wind instruments and suggest a variety of sounds combined.*

*As with the melodies, Example 3 is presented first with just the notes and then with the dynamics and articulations added.*

*You can also create your own dynamic changes by means of the volume control on your synthesizer. This parameter may also be controlled by a mod wheel or foot pedal. If your synthesizer has touch-sensitive keys, you can experiment with different attacks and decays, as well as with changes during the steady-state phase of the sound.*

# TWO

# The Notational System

## MUSIC IN WESTERN CULTURE

The culture of any society is measured in large degree by the richness of its arts—poetry, painting, and music among them. Music in particular seems to fulfill a most basic human creative impulse and so appears early on in a civilization's development. Music is the logical accompaniment to ritual; whether religion or magic or pure wonder, music has been used to express those thoughts and feelings that transcend the mere verbal.

The exact form and expression that music takes vary from culture to culture. Some find their highest expression in song and develop it to a high degree of sophistication; other cultures aspire to symphonies.

The comparative study of the music of different cultures is called *ethnomusicology* and is a fascinating study. Unfortunately, in this book we must concentrate on just one small area—Western music from roughly the end of the seventeenth century to our own day. Western music is principally that of Western European culture; we will touch only briefly on music of other cultures, in those specific instances of influence or cross-fertilization.

One of the glories of any culture is that sense of common heritage. Regardless of our nationality or language, we can share in works of art. Beethoven was German but was known all over Europe in his own day. In our day, his works are played and enjoyed worldwide. Musical ideas travel freely and know no borders; our contemporary star performers from concert pianists to pop singers are internationally known. Music is truly a universal language.

# WRITTEN MUSIC

Let's follow that last thought a bit further. If we want to read a novel by Thomas Mann in its original language, we must know German; similarly, if we wish to read Voltaire untranslated, we must know French. But once we know the mechanics of music notation we can just as easily read a piece of music by Schubert (Austrian) or by Debussy (French) or Mussorgsky (Russian). It's all the same, at least as far as the notes themselves go.

We can be thankful for that, but we must also appreciate the fact that it might not be so. Certainly, a system of notation, while useful, is not absolutely necessary. Most primitive cultures get along nicely without it and certain traditions—those we generally call folk art—still rely on aural transmission and are stored, so to speak, in the people's collective memory. Much of popular music and jazz is largely improvised or uses so-called head arrangements, and is only later transcribed into written form.

Well, why have a written tradition then? You are probably familiar with what happens to a rumor as it gets spread around. It often comes back in considerably altered form. The same is true of music handed down by aural tradition. Each generation "remembers" slightly differently, and each performer is free to add embellishments. Thus, no *absolute* version of a folksong can be said to exist. This works reasonably well with folksongs, but problems arise when the music becomes more complex.

Historically, the impetus toward notation was supplied by our Western penchant for **polyphony**—the combining of several melodic lines simultaneously. In order for this to be successful, the several voice parts must be coordinated, and the lines must stay reasonably the same every time. A system of notation provides a close if not exact means of indicating the composer's intentions. Once established, it allows an unprecedented expansion of musical expression in form, content, and length. Imagine trying to teach a chorus and orchestra even one chorus of Handel's *Messiah* by *rote,* that is, by singing each and every part until the performer had it memorized! Instead, with music notation we have a record of how Handel himself conceived the piece, and we can reproduce and enjoy that creation for centuries to come.

# MUSIC—A TEMPORAL ART

We said above that music notation was a close but not exact representation of the actual music. Why this is so becomes clearer if we consider the unique nature of music.

As we have seen, music is, first of all, *sound.* Music is intended to be heard. This may seem a strange statement in a book about reading and writing music, but we must never forget that notation is only a means of getting the music from the composer to the listener, by way of the performer.

In Chapter 1, we said that all music is sound unfolding in time. All sounds, from the most simple to the highly complex, have *duration,* that is, they last a specific amount of time, varying from a fraction of a second to several minutes. When the music stops, it is gone in the physical sense and remains only in our memory. You can't leisurely observe a symphony in the same way you can observe a piece of sculpture or a painting. You *can* study a **score**—the written version—of a symphony, but that can never be the same as hearing the symphony. Like drama, our enjoyment of a piece of music relies on our remembering what we have heard and relating that to current and subsequent musical events. Music is a *temporal* art form, and it follows that the devices for organizing musical time are very important. These devices come under the general heading of **rhythm** and will be discussed in detail in the Chapters 3, 5, and 8.

Translating these often complex combinations of sounds and durations into a system of symbols is no small accomplishment. Our system of notation has evolved somewhat willy-nilly over the centuries and is still changing and adapting to meet the ever-changing nature of the music itself. But no matter how sophisticated the notation, there are still *interpretive* decisions that are left to the performer. It is interesting to hear how much two performances of the same piece can differ—even when played by the same performer! Music notation is not unlike a map or key; it is but a guide to the ultimate re-creation of a work of art.

## NOTES AND RESTS

Any notation system, then, consists of symbols that represent specific aspects of the sound we hear—principally pitch and duration. These symbols are given names so that we can verbalize the manifold relationships that exist among the sound events themselves.

The basic symbol is the **note.** By using several different but related symbols, we can represent varying but mathematically related values.

All sounds have specific durations from quite short to very long. Typically, in any piece of music there are a variety of durations, and one set of symbols must be flexible enough to indicate these durations with reasonable precision. The note with the largest value that is still commonly

used is the whole note, an oval shape (called the **notehead**) that is slightly tilted: ☉. There is a value called a double whole note (also occasionally
called a breve), which is written either as a bracketed whole note or as a
square note:

‖O‖       ⊟

This note is no longer in common use.

Other values are derived by a process of simple binary division. A
whole note divides into two half notes: ♩ ♩. The half note is the same
oval head with a **stem** attached. The stem may go up or down, depending
on context.* Observe on which side of the head the stem is attached in
each case. Two half notes equal one whole note in value.

♩ + ♩ = O

Half notes are divided into quarter notes: ♩ ♩. Here the notehead is
filled in. Two quarter notes equal one half note; four quarters equal one
whole note.

♩ + ♩ = ♩ ,      ♩ + ♩ + ♩ + ♩ = O

Quarter notes are divided into eighth notes: ♪ ♪. The curved line to the
right is called a **flag.** Notice that it always goes to the right.

Eighth notes are divided into sixteenth notes ♬, sixteenths into thirty-
second notes ♬, and so on, simply adding additional flags. With groups of
flagged notes, the flags may be replaced with a single **beam:**

♪♪ = ♫   ♬♬♬ = ♬

For every note value, there is a companion symbol that is used to represent a specific duration of silence. These symbols are called **rests.** As
we will see, rests "count" just as much as the notes themselves. Here are
the note values along with their comparable rests:

*See page 22.

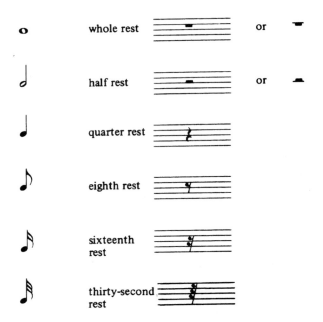

We now have a basic set of symbols. Additional values can be notated by using the dot and the tie. Placing a **dot** after the notehead adds *half* the value of the note:

Rests may also be dotted:

A second dot adds half the value of the first dot:

A dotted note can, of course, be divided into three equal values. Additionally, a dotted note can be divided into two equal values, each of which will itself be a dotted note:

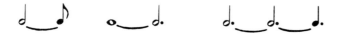

A **tie** joins the values of two or more notes into one longer value:

Up to this point we have defined durations only in relation to other durations (for example, a quarter note is half as long as a half note). The actual length of notes in clock time will take us into a discussion of the way musical time is organized, which we will cover in the next chapter.

## Computer Exercise

Chapter 2    The Notational System
Rhythm Notation
  1.  Note Values (Names & Equivalents)    Drill #2
  2.  Note Values (Including Dots & Ties)—All Levels    Drills #3–6
  3.  Rests—All Levels    Drills #7–9

## Written Exercises

*Once you have mastered the computer drills, work out the following exercises. It is important to master the skills of both reading and writing music, and it may take some practice before your notes and rests appear uniform.*

1.  Identify the indicated note parts:

2. On the line below, write the indicated values. Take care to place the
   noteheads squarely on the line. Stems may go in either direction in
   this instance but should be positioned on the correct side of the notehead and perpendicular to the horizontal line, not leaning. Draw the
   flags neatly and with care. The flags should be curved around to meet
   the stem.

   a. half note      b. eighth note      c. quarter note      d. sixteenth note

   e. dotted quarter note

3. Duration equivalents: Indicate the number of notes of a given value
   that it would take to equal a second value. For example:

   $\underline{2}$ ♩ = 𝅗𝅥

   a.

   ___ ♩ = 𝅗𝅥          ___ 𝅘𝅥𝅯 = ♪
   ___ ♪ = 𝅗𝅥          ___ 𝅘𝅥𝅰 = 𝅘𝅥𝅯
   ___ ♪ = ♩          ___ 𝅘𝅥𝅰 = ♪
   ___ 𝅘𝅥𝅯 = ♩          ___ ♪ = 𝅗𝅥
   ___ 𝅗𝅥 = 𝅝          ___ 𝅘𝅥𝅰 = ♩
   ___ ♩ = 𝅝          ___ ♪ = 𝅝

   b.

   ___ ♩ = ♩.          ___ 𝅗𝅥. = 𝅗𝅥.
   ___ ♪ = 𝅗𝅥.          ___ ♪. = 𝅗𝅥.
   ___ ♪ = ♩.          ___ 𝅘𝅥𝅯 = 𝅗𝅥.
   ___ 𝅘𝅥𝅯 = ♪.          ___ ♪ = 𝅗𝅥.
   ___ ♩ = 𝅝.          ___ 𝅗𝅥. = 𝅝.

c.

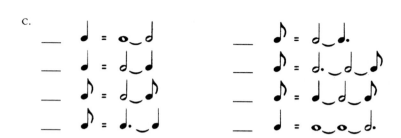

4. On the line below, write the indicated rests. Center the rests on the line. Observe whether the rest sits on the line (half rest) or under the line (whole rest).

a. half rest        b. quarter rest        c. whole rest        d. eighth rest

e. sixteenth rest

5. Duration equivalents using rests: Indicate the number of notes or rests of a specified value that are contained in the given combinations of notes and rests. For example:

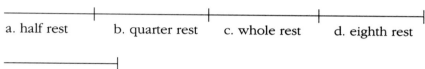

# LETTER-NAMES FOR PITCHES

Pitch notation requires a means of designating the individual sounds and differentiating their **register.** For names, we use the first seven letters of the alphabet, A through G, which are cyclically repeated.

For pitch notation, our now-familiar note shapes are placed on a **staff.** A staff consists of five parallel lines and the spaces in between. For reference, lines and spaces are numbered from the bottom up.

The specific letter-names for notes on the lines and spaces are established by **clef** signs. There are three clefs in common use: treble or G clef, bass or F clef, and C clef. As the names suggest, each clef fixes a certain pitch letter-name on a certain staff line.

The treble clef is in fact a highly modified script G. Note the similarity:

The curlicue at the base of the clef denotes the second line as G.

All the other lines and spaces now have pitch letter-names:

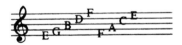

There are many clever mnemonic devices for remembering the lines: *Every Good Boy Deserves Favor,* for example. You may know some others. If not, it might be fun to invent some new ones.

The treble clef is used for higher sounds, such as those produced by violins, flutes, and the upper register of the piano. The word *treble* originally designated a high voice.

The bass clef is likewise a modified script F:

When placed on a staff, it denotes the fourth line as F:

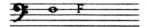

As a result, the lines and spaces in bass clef have different names. You can remember the lines with *Good Boys Do Fine Always* and the spaces with *All Cows Eat Grass.*

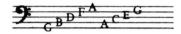

Learning to read music requires knowing both clefs and being able to keep them distinct. With practice, both will become familiar to you.

The bass clef is used for lower sounds, such as those produced by trombones, tubas, cellos, string basses, men's voices, and the lower registers of the piano.

The spaces above and below the staff are routinely used, and the staff can be extended by the use of **ledger lines,** small lines the width of a notehead that in effect continue the lines of the staff:

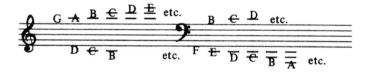

However, use of more than four ledger lines can make reading difficult. Pitches lying even higher or lower can be indicated by the symbol *8ᵛᵃ,* which stands for *octava.* The root stem of *octave* translates as *eight;* the letter-name eight degrees away from any pitch is the same:

| A | B | C | D | E | F | G | A |
|---|---|---|---|---|---|---|---|
| 1 | 2 | 3 | 4 | 5 | 6 | 7 | 8 |

So, these two pitches are identical:

But the first one is easier to read. *8ᵛᵃ* can be used to indicate very low pitches as well, and the *8ᵛᵃ* is written under the notes:

8va (or 8va bassa)

A series of pitches, even entire portions of melodies, can be written *8va*:

The C clef denotes a given line as the letter C. Unlike the G and F clefs, the C clef is movable and may designate the third line as C (alto clef):

or the fourth line as C (tenor clef):

C clefs are used by midrange instruments such as violas, which routinely read in alto clef. Cellos, trombones, and bassoons use the tenor clef when the music falls in their upper registers. Use of the appropriate clef allows most of the music to be notated on the staff, eliminating the cumbersome necessity of using many ledger lines.

The different clefs give us a complete system for indicating precisely the relative highness or lowness of any pitch. Within a given clef, the higher the symbol *appears* on the staff, the higher will be the actual sound.

The following convention is observed for notes having stems: If the note lies below the third line, the stem goes up; if the note lies on or above the third line, the stem goes down.

Where a group of beamed notes appears, the stem direction is governed by where the majority of the notes lie.

Single staves are routinely used for the voice parts of songs and for individual instruments, where the total range from low to high can be accommodated. In situations where the pitches cover a very wide range, as with the piano, a treble and a bass clef are combined into a **great** or **grand staff:**

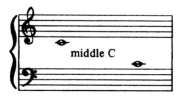

middle C

The two staves have a nice symmetry. Note the placement of the indicated C. This C is known as **middle C,** and in a sense it comes right between the two staves. Because of the distance between the two staves, however, this C must be placed closer to one staff or the other, as in the illustration. Ledger lines can be used above and below either of the staves, though for practical reasons fewer are used in between the staves. Typically, lines will simply pass from one staff to the other:

For vocal or instrumental ensembles, several staves may be braced together into a **system.**

Solo voice or instrument
with piano accompaniment

String quartet

Violin I

Violin II

Viola

Cello

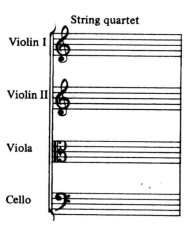

## Computer Exercise

Chapter 2   The Notational System
Pitch Notation
1. Pitch Naming—All Levels (Tenor & Alto Clefs Optional)    Drills #10–19
2. Pitch Writing—All Levels (Tenor & Alto Clefs Optional)    Drills #20–24

# REGISTERS OF THE PIANO

For ease in reference, the gamut of pitches (illustrated here with the
piano keyboard) is divided into specific registers, each consisting of seven
pitches from C to B. Following is the range of the piano, notated conventionally on a great staff, with the appropriate registral designations and
the system of letter designations:

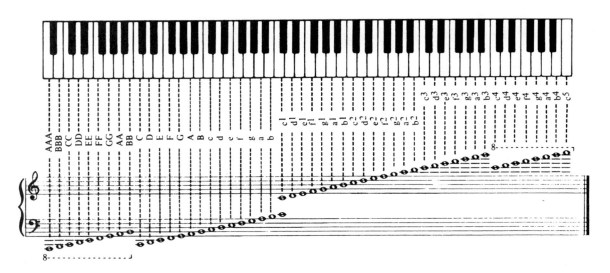

## Computer Exercise

Chapter 2   The Notational System
Pitch Notation
3. Piano Keyboard    Drill #25

## Written Exercises

*As before, after mastering the computer drills, work out the following written exercises.*

1. Write the letter-name for each of the following pitches, using the correct registral designations:

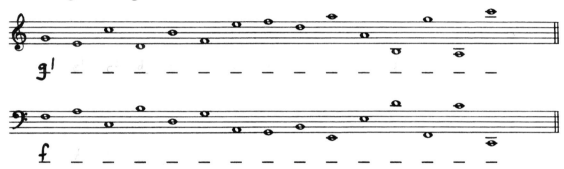

2. Write the notes indicated by the letter-names at the appropriate place on the great staff. Use ledger lines or *8ᵛᵃ* as needed. Take care that the noteheads are placed clearly on the appropriate line or in the appropriate space.

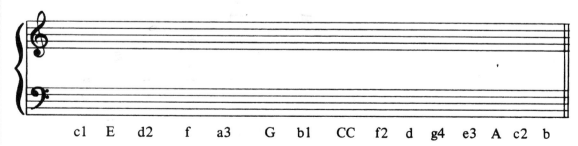

c1   E   d2   f   a3   G   b1   CC   f2   d   g4   e3   A   c2   b

3. Rewrite this melody in bass clef in the register indicated by the first note. Stem directions may need to be changed, depending on where the notes fall on the staff. Be sure the stems go on the correct side of the note. Whenever writing music, work for neatness, clarity, and legibility.

4. Rewrite this melody in treble clef, following the directions for Exercise 3. Register is indicated by the first note.

# Notation at the Computer

*When music was primarily written by hand, it was considered vital that the notation be clear and easy to read. Most clean copy was done by scribes or, later, by experts in musical calligraphy. The invention of printing made it possible to reproduce extremely legible copies of the music, but much was still hand-copied. It was always recommended that the copyist use black ink and a beveled-nib pen on heavy paper for the best results. The past decade has seen the development of sophisticated computer software for music notation. Such programs as Coda Technology's Finale® and Music Pro's Nightingale®*

*have given everybody with a computer and a laser printer the capabilty for desktop music publishing.*

*If you have one of these notation programs installed, you may wish to do the last four exercises at the computer. The printed copy will certainly be legible! At the same time, the use of these programs will give you additional practice in the manipulation of the various notational symbols. Since the computer will do only what you direct it to do, you must select exactly the right symbols for both pitch and duration. As with the drills for this book, the computer is patient and forgiving, but you've got to "get it right" or you will get the dreaded error messages!*

# THREE
# Simple Meter

## Suggested Listening

*Listen to several selections of music designed for movement, such as marches or dance music. These may be drawn from a wide spectrum of periods and styles, including the latest in popular music. Notice your physical response to the music. What characteristics of the music elicit this response? Do you react especially to any particular instruments or any particular element in the music? As before, don't be concerned if your responses are very general.*

## THE BEAT

Rhythm is the most basic element of music. It is hard to conceive of music that is pitches only, with no sense of rhythm whatever, but we can easily imagine rhythms without pitches. In fact, we can recognize many pieces just by their rhythmic patterns alone, and it follows that rhythm is an important element in making music memorable.

When listening to a piece of music, notice your physical reaction to the rhythm. If you are like most people, you will end up tapping your foot or otherwise moving in time to the music. You are responding to the *beat* of the music.

We define the **beat** as a series of pulses or segments of musical time that are even, regular, and ongoing. The beat is a reference point for all the varied durations of the notes. The beat is something we feel, though in some cases it may be made quite explicit. (When you listen to the drums in a marching band or jazz band, the bass drum likely will be playing the beat.)

The durations of the sounds themselves may be equivalent to the value of the beat; they may be several beats long, or there may be several notes to each beat. We tend to feel the beat as the value somewhere between the longest notes and the shortest. Since this is a psychological response, individuals may differ in their perception of the beat. We will observe also that the speed or pace of the beat varies from piece to piece. The rate of the beat is called **tempo** and is indicated either by reference to a metronome or by terms describing the speed or character of the piece. We will encounter these terms shortly.

Finally, we can designate any note value as the unit of the beat, even dotted note values. A given note achieves a specific duration only when the number and tempo of the underlying beat is established.

Now, music consisting of only beat-length values would be fairly dull; likewise, too wide a variety of different durations will soon begin to sound incoherent. What is needed is a rational and perceivable organizational scheme for relating and understanding (as well as limiting) the variety of durations presented by any piece of music. This structural scheme we call **meter.**

## THE ORGANIZATION OF MUSIC INTO METERS

If we tap or clap an extended series of beats at a moderate tempo, we begin to notice a tendency to differentiate or organize the beats into patterns marked by regularly recurring accent or stress. These patterns generally follow one of two possibilities—every other beat or every third beat accented. We may feel these accented beats as stronger or subtly louder. It would be like writing the notes as follows:

or

If we then separate these patterns by vertical lines, we have a series of **measures** or **bars** of two or three beats each:

The dividing lines are naturally called **barlines.** Our term *meter,* in fact, comes from the Greek word meaning "to measure."

This metric pattern then becomes the basis for organizing the rhythms or varied durations of the piece. As a convenience, we indicate the meter or accent pattern to be used by a **meter signature,** commonly called a **time signature,** which we place at the beginning of the piece.

A metric pattern having two quarter notes to the measure is indicated by the signature $\frac{2}{4}$. The top number tells us the number of beats in the measure, and the bottom number stands for the unit of the beat, in this case a quarter note. A metric pattern with three quarter notes per measure would be $\frac{3}{4}$. Note that this is *not* a fraction; 3/4 is incorrect.

Both $\frac{2}{4}$ and $\frac{3}{4}$ are examples of **simple meters.** In simple meters, note values are routinely combined or divided in multiples of two. The following combinations are typical:

There is an extraordinary diversity of rhythmic patterns here. Almost any combination of note values is possible, as long as the values within the measure add up to the value indicated by the meter signature. In actual practice, the composer tends to limit the number and complexity of the patterns in any given piece.

Usually, when eighth notes and smaller values are used within a beat they are beamed together. This makes the music easier to read. Individual flags are used only in vocal music where a note takes a single syllable of the text. Dotted notes can be used but must not obscure the basic meter. In the following example, the written notation is read as if the dot substitutes for the tie:

**written:**      **read:**

Meters having four beats to the measure are also commonly found. In a sense, one measure of $\frac{4}{4}$ is not unlike two measures of $\frac{2}{4}$, though a subtle distinction is sometimes made between beat one (primary accent) and beat three (secondary accent). (In most music written before about 1750, the first and third beats are generally considered as equivalent.) All the combinations of $\frac{2}{4}$ are found in $\frac{4}{4}$, with these additionally:

Since any note value can be designated the unit of the beat, we have a large number of possible meters. For sake of easy comparison, we group them by the number of beats:

simple duple: $\frac{2}{2}$ or $\mathbb{C}$, $\frac{2}{4}$, $\frac{2}{8}$, $\frac{2}{16}$, etc.

simple triple: $\frac{3}{2}$, $\frac{3}{4}$, $\frac{3}{8}$, $\frac{3}{16}$, etc.

simple quadruple: $\frac{4}{2}$, $\frac{4}{4}$ or $\mathbf{c}$, $\frac{4}{8}$, etc.

Remember, a lower number of 2 stands for a half note, 4 for a quarter note, 8 for an eighth note, and so on. The symbols $\mathbf{c}$ and $\mathbb{C}$ are a holdover from an earlier system of meter signatures. $\mathbb{C}$ means *alla breve* and designates the half note as the unit of the beat; $\mathbf{c}$ is often incorrectly taken to stand for "common" time but is interchangeable with $\frac{4}{4}$. It is also theoretically possible to have the whole note as the unit of the beat, e.g., $\frac{4}{1}$.

Ends of sections within a larger composition, and occasionally shorter subdivisions, are set off by the use of a double barline: ‖. This is a means of musical "punctuation." The end of a composition is indicated by the use of a double barline having one thin and one thick barline: ▐.

## Computer Exercise

## Written Exercises

*Add barlines in the appropriate places for the given meter signature. Place a double barline at the end of each example. The first note or rest is always the first beat of the measure.*

# RHYTHM IN PERFORMANCE

We indicated earlier that the note values we use are all relative and thus have no *absolute* value or duration. In performance, the actual "real time" duration of any note is determined by first establishing a tempo for the beat. Once the value of the beat unit is defined, all the relative values are in turn specifically defined.

Selecting the proper tempo for a piece of music can be quite subjective. Until the invention of the metronome, tempo was generally determined by the average note value (lots of "fast" notes implied a fast tempo) or by some designation as to the character of the piece (e.g., a dance movement or march or lament). Some of these terms, such as *allegro,* which in Italian means lively or merrily, now have commonly understood connotations of tempo—in this case, fast. Other examples include *grave,* which means serious or somber and implies a slow tempo, and *largo,* meaning broad or wide, again implying a slow tempo. Other terms were gradually adopted that had more to do with the pace of the beat: *andante,* from the Italian *andare* (to go), which means literally a "walking" tempo; *moderato* (moderately, thus neither slow nor fast); *presto* (very quickly); *tempo guisto* (measure the time precisely and evenly), and so forth.

Here are the most common terms, ordered from slowest to fastest. Others will be found in the Glossary.

*grave*—seriously; thus a slow, solemn tempo
*adagio*—slower than andante; quite slow
*andante*—walking tempo; usually interpreted as slow
*andantino*—literally, a little andante; faster than andante
*moderato*—moderately; neither too fast nor too slow
*allegretto*—literally, a little allegro; slower than allegro
*allegro*—bright and cheerful, thus a fairly quick tempo
*vivace*—lively; a very quick tempo
*presto*—a quick tempo
*prestissimo*—the superlative degree; about as fast as possible

The metronome allowed the composer to indicate tempos exactly in relation to clock time by specifying so many beats per minute. For example, M.M. (standing for Maelzel's Metronome) 60 means that 60 beats should occur in a minute's time; M.M. 96 means 96 beats per minute; M.M. 136 means 136 beats per minute.

Experience tells us that it is very difficult to maintain an absolutely precise tempo throughout a piece. As the music gets more exciting, we tend to speed up a little, and as it relaxes we slow down. Composers can indicate a flexibility of tempo by the use of the term **rubato,** which literally means to rob from the time by now holding back and speeding to "catch up."

The composer may wish to markedly change the tempo. The term *accelerando* (abbreviated *accel.*) means to speed up; *ritard* (abbreviated *rit.*) means to slow down. *Poco a poco* (literally, little by little) means gradually. *A tempo* signifies the resumption of a steady tempo following any tempo fluctuation.

This next computer exercise covers some of these terms and introduces some new terms. If you aren't familiar with all the terms, review their definitions in the Glossary.

## Computer Exercise

Chapter 12    Looking at Music
   1. Musical Terms—Tempo Indications    Drill #156

## COUNTING TIME IN SIMPLE METERS

Sometimes it must seem that musicians spend the greatest part of their lives counting. Counting is the surest way we have of establishing the durational relationships of the notes and performing them evenly and correctly.

There are numerous counting systems, all of which supply a verbal equivalent for each metric unit. We count the beats by number:

For notes of several beats' duration, we vocalize the count only where notes occur, but we must keep the beat going to ensure precision and uniformity in the note values. We can do this by tapping or clapping the pulse while vocalizing, or we can conduct the metric pattern.

Simple divisions can be done most simply thus:

one  and  two  and    one  and  two  and    | etc.

Subdivisions can be counted like this:

one - e  and - a  two - e  and - a

Here is an example fully counted:

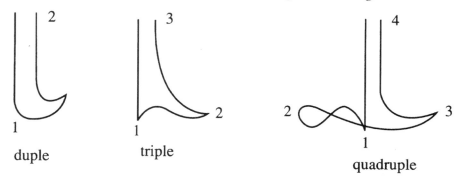

In most large and small ensembles, it falls to the conductor to "count," or to keep track of the meter, through a beat pattern described by the conductor's baton. Here are the patterns for duple, triple, and quadruple meters. You may wish to use them while doing the counting drills below.

The first beat of every measure is called the **downbeat.** This term derives from the conductor's beat pattern, in which the motion for beat one is always straight down. The remaining beats in the measure, and particularly the last beat, are called **upbeats.** It is not at all unusual for rhythmic patterns to begin on an upbeat. A partial measure prior to the first downbeat is called an **anacrusis** or simply a **pickup;** it may be as short as a fraction of a beat or as long as three beats, depending on the meter. One standard convention says that the value of this upbeat is deducted from the final measure (making that measure incomplete), but this convention is not always rigorously followed.

Here are some examples of rhythmic patterns beginning with upbeats or anacruses:

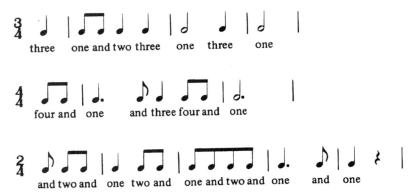

We have seen that ties must be used to create durations which can't be expressed by a single note, dotted or otherwise, or values which span the barline. A note may even have a duration lasting for several measures. (In fact, a note may last as long as the composer desires.) In counting tied notes, we must take care to keep track of the ongoing number of beats contained within the tied value. Here are some examples:

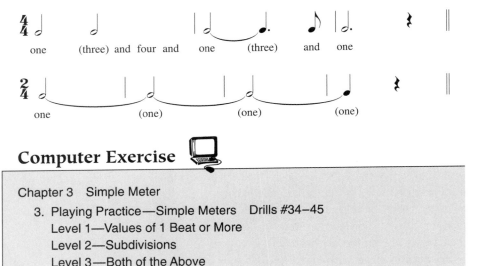

## Computer Exercise

Chapter 3    Simple Meter
  3. Playing Practice—Simple Meters    Drills #34–45
       Level 1—Values of 1 Beat or More
       Level 2—Subdivisions
       Level 3—Both of the Above

## Music for Study

*Write out and count the rhythms of each of the following melodies. Identify the meter of each. Observe that the meter signature is placed in only the first measure and is not repeated on subsequent staves. How many beats in a measure? What is the unit of the beat? (You will find any unfamiliar tempo terms defined in the Glossary.) First, count the rhythms aloud, using a neutral pitch. Then, count along as the tune is played or sung.*

## EXAMPLE 1

*"Passing By"*    TRADITIONAL

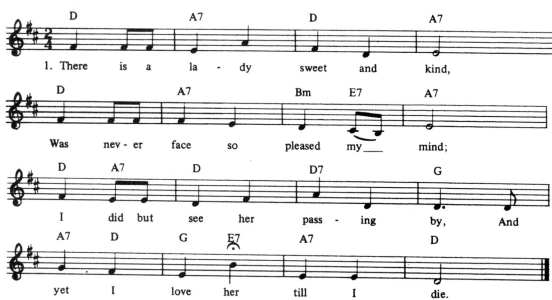

The symbol ⌒ is called a **fermata.** *This symbol means to hold a note beyond its normal value. In practice, it directs a pause or a suspension of the rhythmic flow for a period of time determined by the performer. Short fermatas are used for expressive effect. Fermatas are often referred to colloquially as "bird's eyes," for obvious reasons, or "coronas."*

## EXAMPLE 2

*Symphony No. 7, Second Movement*

LUDWIG VAN BEETHOVEN (1770–1827)

**Allegretto**

**EXAMPLE 3**

*"Follow the Leader"*    BÉLA BARTÓK (1881–1945)

**EXAMPLE 4**

*"The Ash Grove"*    WELSH FOLKSONG

The ash grove how__ grace - ful, how plain - ly__ 'tis__ speak - ing; The

wind thro'__ it__ play - ing has lan - guage for me.

**EXAMPLE 5**

*"Polovetzian Dance"*    ALEXANDER BORODIN (1833–1887)

**EXAMPLE 6**

*"Deck the Halls"*    OLD WELSH AIR

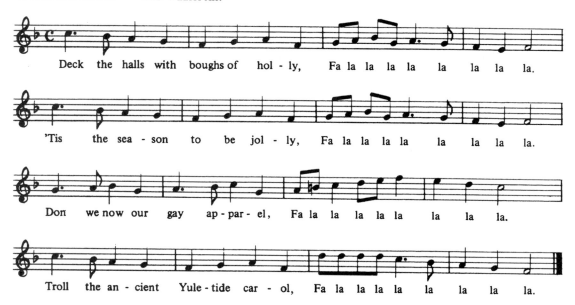

Deck the halls with boughs of hol - ly, Fa la la la la    la    la la    la.

'Tis    the sea - son    to    be jol - ly, Fa la la la la    la    la la    la.

Don    we now our    gay ap - par - el, Fa la la    la la la    la    la la.

Troll    the an - cient    Yule - tide car - ol, Fa la la la la    la    la la    la.

**EXAMPLE 7**

*"The Merry Farmer"*    ROBERT SCHUMANN (1810–1856)

Allegro animato

**EXAMPLE 8**

*Sonatina, Op. 36, No. 1, Rondo*    MUZIO CLEMENTI (1752–1832)

Spiritoso

**EXAMPLE 9**

*"Ave Maria"*    CHARLES GOUNOD (1818–1893)

Andante con moto

**EXAMPLE 10**

*"Dixie"*    DANIEL EMMETT (1815–1904)

I___ wish I was_ in the land of cot - ton, Old times there are

not for-got ten, Look a - way! Look a - way! Look a - way! Dix - ie Land.

# Music for Study: Counting with Rests

*We have observed that the beat is felt to continue steadily under the music, regardless of the actual note values being used, even when the beat is only very subtly implied. In fact, so strong is the sense of the beat, we feel it even during brief stretches where there is no sound at all. It follows that rests must be counted as strictly as the notes themselves:*

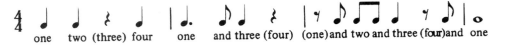

one   two (three) four     one    and three (four)  (one) and two and three (four) and one

*Count the rhythms in the following melodies. As before, first just count, using a neutral pitch. Then, count along as the melodies are played or sung. Tap the beat to assure rhythmic accuracy with the rests.*

**EXAMPLE 1**

*"Springtime Song"*    BÉLA BARTÓK (1881–1945)

Andante

**EXAMPLE 2**

*Sarabande*    GEORGE FREDERICK HANDEL (1685–1759)

**EXAMPLE 3**

*Little Prelude No. 1*    JOHANN SEBASTIAN BACH (1685–1750)

**EXAMPLE 4**

*Air*    GEORGE FREDERICK HANDEL (1685–1759)

Rests are also used simply to shorten the value of notes coming on the beat. Here the rests would not be counted, strictly speaking, but would tell the performer to release the note on the second half of each beat.

**EXAMPLE 5**

*"Soldier's March"*    ROBERT SCHUMANN (1810–1856)

Allegro

# THE USE OF BEAMS

You may have noticed that beams are a tremendous aid to the eye in seeing the metric organization of the measure, quickly locating the beat, and easily parsing the divisions of the beat. For this reason, most music makes use of beamed groups rather than using single flags. The one general exception to this is vocal music, where the individual flags are used to indicate where the syllables of the text fall, but even there it is becoming much more common to use the beams.

Beams should be used to group any and all small values falling *within* a beat:

In meters like $\frac{2}{4}$, $\frac{3}{4}$, and $\frac{4}{4}$, beams may connect notes of like value from one beat to the next:

An entire measure of shorter meters can be combined under one beam, but notes in a "long" meter like $\frac{4}{4}$ are routinely combined in half measures.

Beams should always reflect the meter. Incorrect beaming:

Correct beaming—notice the clarity of the individual beats:

## Written Exercises

1.  Replace individual flags with beams wherever possible.

2. Complete the following measures. You may use a single note or several notes, as is appropriate.

Given:

One possible solution:

3. Complete the last measure of each given example. Remember that the value of the upbeat is subtracted from the value of the final measure.

Given:

Solution:

# Computer Exercise

Chapter 3   Simple Meter
  4. Rhythmic Composition—Simple Meters   Drill #46

## Creating Rhythms at the Computer

*You will be given a meter signature with four empty bars and a limited number of rhythmic values from which to choose. When creating your rhythms, start with simple patterns that are coherent and clearly imply the meter (putting longer notes on metric accents, for example). Strive for movement across the barline. It is not necessary (or even desirable) to avoid repetition, but you should have some variety. End your patterns with longer notes, those of a full measure or at least a half measure in duration. The computer will then play back your patterns. If you have incomplete measures or measures with too many notes, the computer will prompt you to try again.*

# Scales

## HALF STEPS AND WHOLE STEPS

In the discussion of the overtone series in Chapter 1, we cited the importance of the octave, with its unique acoustical "sameness" and its consequent structural significance in defining a given register and providing the "boundary" or framing interval for scales.

Theoretically, we could divide the octave into any number of smaller intervals. The scientist uses a standard division into 100 increments (called **cents**) for purposes of making fine distinctions in the size or **tuning** of musical intervals. Musicians are very concerned about good **intonation,** or playing in tune. This refers to the ability to match pitches and to play pitches neither sharp (too high) nor flat (too low). For practical reasons, music uses a much smaller number of intervals. The usual number is 12 equal increments, though some folk music and contemporary music uses up to 24.

To see this standard division, it helps to look at a piano keyboard. We notice a pattern of seven white and five black keys that repeats in each octave or register:

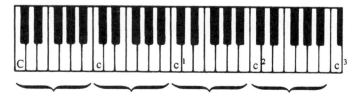

The smallest increment is represented by adjacent keys, either white to black or, in two cases, white to white. This interval is called a **semitone**

or **half step.** By skipping a key, we find the interval of a **tone** or **whole step.** Most scales are basically composed of whole steps and half steps.

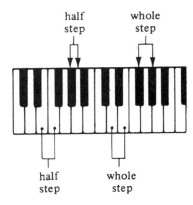

# Computer Exercise

Chapter 4    Scales
Whole Steps and Half Steps
   1. Whole Steps & Half Steps on the Keyboard    Drill #47

The ability to *hear* the elements of music is as important as the ability to read and write them. To this end, the instruction page for computer drills #47 and #48 gives you the opportunity to listen to the sound of the whole step and the half step. Additionally, as you do the drills, the computer will play back your response for every problem. *Listen carefully* as you work.

Up to this point, we have been using only the pitches represented by the white keys on the piano.

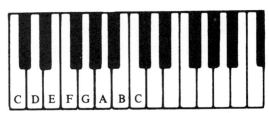

Even though there are only five black keys, they give us a total of ten additional pitches. Each black key can represent both a raising of one white key pitch or a lowering of another. If we move to the right from a white key (say, C) to the immediately adjacent black key, we say we have raised the pitch a half step. We place a symbol, called a **sharp,** in front of the note and call the new note C sharp (C♯):

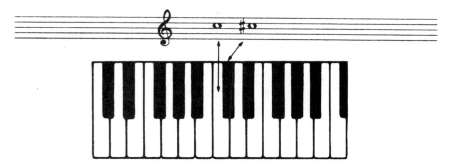

Similarly, if we move to the left (say, from E), we say we have lowered the pitch a half step. We place a symbol, called a **flat,** in front of the note and call the new note E flat (E♭):

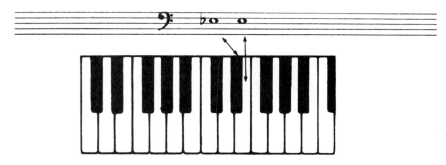

Curiously, even though the sharp or flat goes in front of the note in the music itself, we say it *after* the letter, as in A *flat* or G *sharp*. There is a common tendency at first to get mixed up and put the sharp or flat after the note in the music:

Check yourself. The sharp or flat always goes in front of the note.

We can now identify all notes of the keyboard, noting that each black key normally represents *two* pitches.

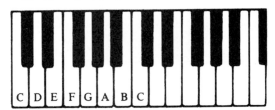

We can notate whole steps by indicating the notes that would lie on nonadjacent keys on the piano. This may be a white key to a white key, a black key to a black key, white to black, or black to white, all depending on where the keys are. On the staff, however, a whole step will always be from a space to the next higher or lower line, or from a line to the next higher or lower space.

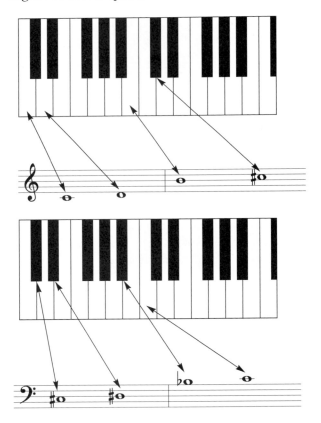

Whole steps must always be spelled with adjacent letter names. E♮ to F♯ is a whole step, but E♮ to G♭, even though played on the same keys of the piano, is not.

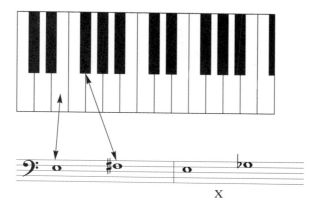

Pitches that are named differently but are played on the same keys of the piano are called **enharmonic.** Examples are A♯ and B♭, E♭ and D♯, and so on.

We can also see now that there are two ways of notating a half step on the keyboard: by using the same letter-name, for example C to C♯; by using the adjacent letter-name, for example C to D♭. The half step involving two letter-names is called a **diatonic half step** and is the form found in almost all scales. That with the same letter-name is called a **chromatic half step** and is found only in the chromatic scale. Which we choose is based on the context of the music. Here is one example:

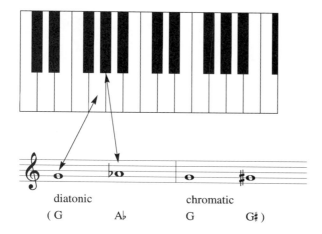

# Computer Exercise

There are actually five symbols that we use to represent raised or lowered pitches. These symbols are called **accidentals.** In addition to the sharp and flat are the **natural sign** (♮), which cancels another accidental; the **double sharp** (𝄪), which raises a sharped note another half step; and the **double flat** (𝄫), which lowers a flatted note another half step.

Accidentals can be applied to any note. If we take the note B and sharp it, we have B sharp (B♯). This note is played on the key we normally call C, since the adjacent key to B is another white key. (B♯ and C♮ are enharmonic.)

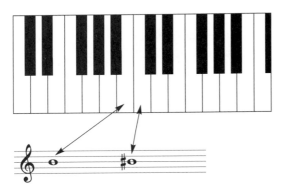

Here are other examples:

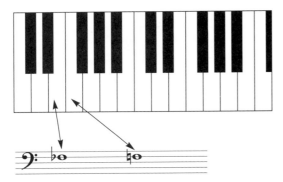

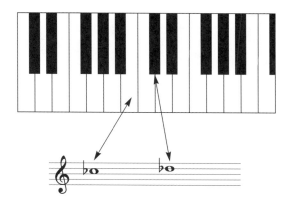

It follows that any letter-name could have five different pitches associated with it. Illustrated with G's, they are:

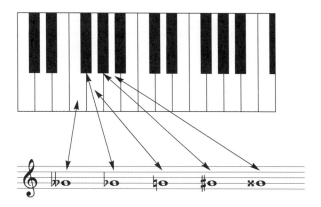

This gives us many more pitches than would appear from just looking at the keyboard, and there are uses for all of them. The apparent discrepancy between the number of named pitches and the number of keys on the piano is accounted for by those enharmonics. We will see that there is a big difference between, say, F♯ and G♭, and on certain instruments the two pitches even have slightly different frequencies and thus pitches. These discrepancies are called **tuning differentials,** and the way the note is written or tuned depends entirely on the context in which that note occurs.

## Computer Exercise

## Written Exercises

*Once you feel you have mastered the computer exercises presented so far in this chapter, do the following:*

1.  Write the note one whole step *above* the given note.

2.  Write the note one whole step *below* the given note.

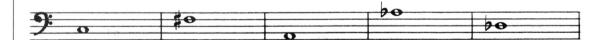

3.  Write the note that is a *diatonic* half step *above*.

4. Write the note that is a *diatonic* half step *below*.

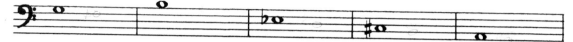

5. Write the note that is a *chromatic* half step *above*.

6. Write the note that is a *chromatic* half step *below*.

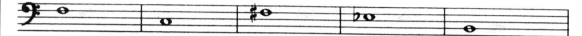

7. Write the note that is *enharmonic* to the given note.

# THE MAJOR SCALE

Here is the music to the familiar tune "Home, Sweet Home":

*"Home, Sweet Home"*    SIR HENRY BISHOP (1786–1855)

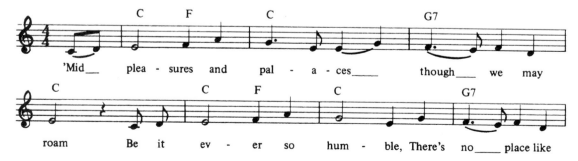

*"Home, Sweet Home,"* continued

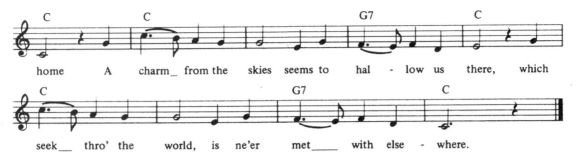

home    A    charm_ from the    skies    seems to    hal - low us    there,    which

seek__ thro' the    world,    is    ne'er    met____ with    else - where.

At first glance, there is much diversity in the music—the total number of pitches, the direction of the line, the various rhythms, and so on. But a closer examination reveals that there are actually only seven different pitches in this piece. It should also be apparent that the composer was very selective in the order and arrangement of those pitches. We sense a plan or a design, and we feel a certain satisfaction or completeness when the song is over.

The techniques whereby the composer organizes the raw pitch material comprise one of the most important areas of musical study.

In the example above, notice particularly the importance of the note C. Not only is it the first pitch and the last pitch, but it is also the highest pitch and the lowest pitch. Thus it acts somewhat as a frame, or point of reference, for the piece. This pitch is called the **key note,** or **tonic,** and the music is said to be *in the key* of that note. The way in which the other pitches relate to C can be more easily studied if we arrange the pitches in ascending order, starting on C.

1    2    3    4    5    6    7    8

For convenience, we number the pitches, or scale degrees, from lowest to highest.

We now have a *scale.* A **scale** is an arrangement of pitches in systematic, ascending order. The term comes from the Italian *scala,* which literally means "steps." There are obviously many scales, and they are differentiated by the specific placement of whole and half steps. This placement, along with all the other note-to-note relationships within the scale, accounts for the particular flavor of music based on a particular scale. We will compare the sounds of various scales as we discuss them in turn.

Returning to the scale derived from "Home, Sweet Home," we find the following pattern of whole steps and half steps:

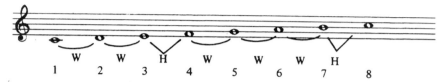

This pattern defines this scale as a **major scale,** and we call this particular scale a C-major scale. We can construct a major scale on any pitch simply by using accidentals to create the necessary whole steps and half steps.

Let's build a major scale on D. If we use just the white notes of the piano, we know our half steps will fall in the wrong places.

Since we need a whole step from scale degree 2 to 3, we raise the F to F♯. This now gives us the needed half step from scale degree 3 to 4. Similarly, by raising C to C♯, we get a whole step from 6 to 7 and a half step from 7 to 8.

Compare the sound of this scale to that of the C-major scale. The D-major scale will sound identical, only a whole step higher.

Let's build a major scale on F. With the white notes, we have a whole step from 3 to 4.

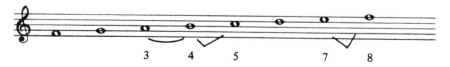

We must make this a half step by *lowering* B to B♭. We now have an F-major scale.

3    4              7    8

Note that the half steps must always be diatonic half steps, that is, use adjacent scale degrees, as in A to B♭. A to A♯ would be incorrect, and in fact would result in the omission of a scale degree!

We can start on raised or lowered notes as well.

In common usage, major scales are found on all of these pitches: C, C♯, D♭, D, E♭, E, F, F♯, G♭, G, A♭, A, B♭, B, and C♭.

A thorough and secure knowledge of scales is basic to all the material that will follow. As an aid in learning the *sound* of the major scale, the instruction page for the major-scale computer exercises includes a demonstration scale. The computer will play the scale as it highlights each note. Listen carefully to this demonstration and also to the playback of the various drills. There are a variety of writing and recognition drills on the computer disk, and you should work with these prior to doing the written exercises. If the written exercises seem difficult or if you encounter problems, return to the computer for additional drill.

## Computer Exercise

Chapter 4   Scales
The Major Scale
   1. Major Scale Writing—All Levels   Drills #53–54
   2. Major Scale Spelling—All Levels   Drills #55–56
   3. Major Scale Recognition—All Levels   Drills #57–60

## Written Exercises

*When you feel you have mastered the computer drills, work out the follow-ing written exercises. As before, these exercises are designed to develop the manual skills of actually writing music and to check your comprehension of the materials away from the computer. Your instructor may ask you to hand in these exercises for purposes of evaluation.*

1. Add accidentals to make the following scales major:

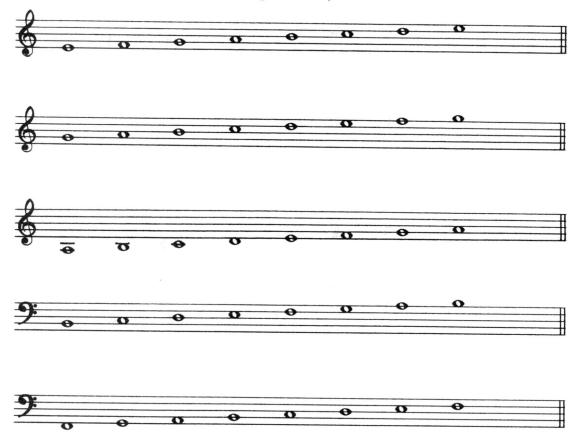

2. Construct major scales on the given pitches, using accidentals as needed. Write your scales in one octave from tonic to tonic. Label whole and half steps.

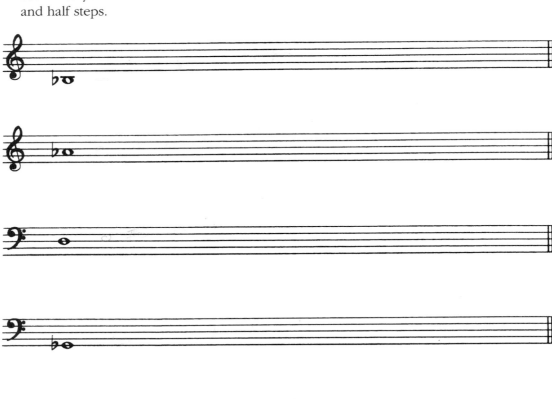

## KEY SIGNATURES FOR MAJOR KEYS

Look at this example of keyboard music written with all accidentals:

*Fugue No. 13 from* The Well-Tempered Clavier, *Book I*

JOHANN SEBASTIAN BACH (1685–1750)

In cases where the same notes are consistently altered throughout a piece, it is far easier to use a *key signature*.

A **key signature** simply takes all the necessary accidentals and places them in a particular order at the beginning of every staff. The following scales illustrate this procedure:

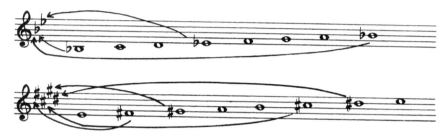

Note that one accidental in a key signature applies to every pitch having that same letter-name, regardless of register.

Because of the importance of key signatures in defining the scale and thus the pitch material of the music, key signatures are placed at the beginning of every staff and are placed on both staves of the grand staff.

The order of sharps and flats in the key signature reflects the relationship of the scales and keys themselves.

If we start with a C-major scale, which has no sharps or flats, and then build a major scale starting on G, the fifth degree, we find that this scale requires one sharp.

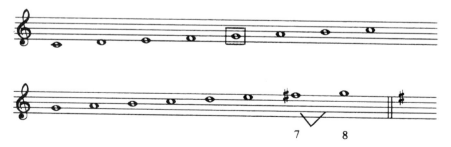

In a like manner, if we built a scale on D, the fifth degree of G major, we find that this scale requires two sharps, and so on.

Here are the key signatures in order of increasing sharps for all major keys with sharps:

Note that in each case the last sharp in the key signature is the seventh degree of the scale, and we can always determine the key note or tonic of any major key by going up one half step from the last sharp.

Let's repeat the same process starting with the C-major scale, but instead going *down* five steps or *up* four steps. Building a major scale on F requires one flat in the signature.

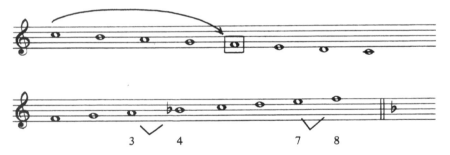

Building a major scale on B♭, five degrees down from F, requires two flats, and so on.

This procedure will give us all the major keys with flats.

Note that in each case the last flat in the signature is for the *fourth* scale degree. To find tonic, merely count down four letter-names; alternatively, with key signatures having more than one flat, the letter-name of the next-to-last flat will be tonic.

Note that the letter order of the flat keys is the reverse of the letter order of the sharp keys and that the letter order of the flats themselves— B E A D G C F—is the reverse of the letter order of the sharps—F C G D A E B.

This ordering of keys five steps apart is often called the **circle of fifths** and is graphically illustrated as follows:

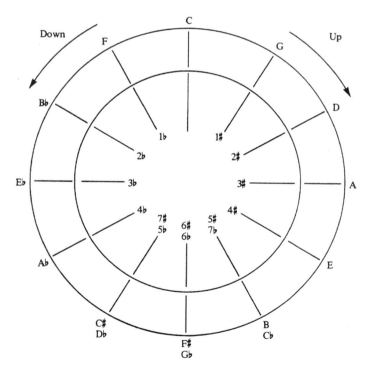

Although theoretically a spiral, the circle is "closed" with those keys that are enharmonic: C♯ and D♭, F♯ and G♭, and B and C♭.

## Computer Exercise

Chapter 4   Scales
Major Key Signatures
1. Major Key Signature Spelling—All Levels    Drills #61–62
2. Major Key Signature Recognition—All Levels    Drills #63–64

## Written Exercises

*When writing key signatures, check to be sure the accidentals are in the proper order and neatly and clearly placed on the correct line or space.*

1. Identify the major keys designated by the following key signatures:

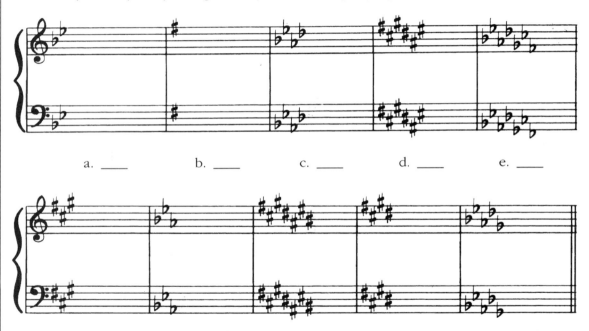

a. ____        b. ____        c. ____        d. ____        e. ____

f. ____        g. ____        h. ____        i. ____        j. ____

2. Write the key signatures for the following major keys:

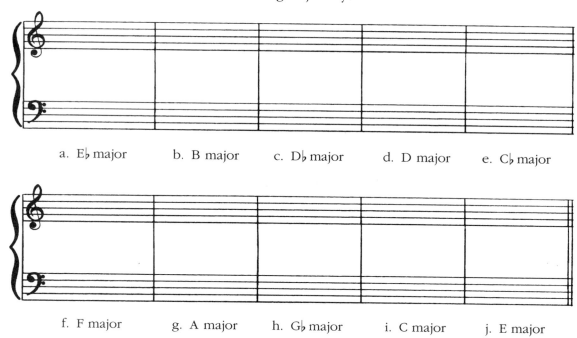

   a. E♭ major     b. B major     c. D♭ major     d. D major     e. C♭ major

   f. F major     g. A major     h. G♭ major     i. C major     j. E major

## INTERVALS IN THE MAJOR SCALE

When we talk about music, we are talking about note *relationships.* These are manifold, and all are important—a given note may be shorter or longer than another, higher or lower, louder or softer. The notes may be close together or far apart; they may be played together or separately.

Any two notes form what we call an **interval;** intervals are the most basic building blocks of musical structures. Intervals have two important properties: *size* and *quality.*

**Size** refers to the distance from one note to another in terms of scale degrees. This distance is designated by an arabic number. Whole steps and diatonic half steps are both technically *seconds,* since both intervals encompass *two* scale degrees. Seconds are symbolized by an arabic 2. The difference between the whole-step second and the half-step second is referred to as **quality,** and is a measurement of the semitone content of the interval. We call the whole step a *major* second, abbreviated M2, since the whole step consists of two half steps; major here means *large* second. We call the half step itself a *minor* second, abbreviated m2; minor here means *small* second. The difference between a major and minor second is, of course, a half step.

Here is a summary of the seconds found in the major scale:

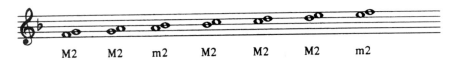

M2     M2     m2     M2     M2     M2     m2

Intervals that encompass three scale degrees are called *thirds* and are symbolized by an arabic 3. Like seconds, the thirds in the major scale are either major or minor.

The third from tonic to the third scale degree in the major mode consists of two whole steps.

W     W     = M3

This third is *major.* The third from scale degrees 2 to 4, however, is only a step and a half.

W     H     = m3

This third is *minor.* And so on, up the scale:

m3    M3    M3    m3    m3

The major thirds are especially important in giving the major scale its "flavor."

In like fashion, an interval encompassing four scale degrees is a *fourth,* five degrees a *fifth,* and so on.

Intervals are an important part of the study of music, and we will devote an entire chapter to them.

# NAMES OF THE SCALE DEGREES

Music that uses predominantly the tones of a given scale and is organized around the tonic pitch is termed **tonal,** and the music is said to be in a **key.** For example, music that uses the G-major scale is said to be in the key of G major; music that uses the E♭-major scale is in the key of E♭ major.

In traditional tonal music, the tones of the scale tend to fall into recognizable and predictable patterns. Understanding the relationships among the various scale degrees is central to a broader understanding of the music itself. The names of the scale degrees give us clues to these relationships.

The first scale degree is the **tonic** and is the pitch toward which all the other pitches gravitate.

The fifth scale degree is called the **dominant.** It is second in importance to the tonic and tends to be a very important structural pitch, along with tonic.

The third scale degree is the **mediant,** so called because it lies halfway between tonic and dominant. These three pitches together outline the **tonic triad.** (Triads will be fully explained in Chapter 10.)

The second scale degree is called the **supertonic,** because it lies one step above the tonic. It frequently acts as a neighbor to the tonic or is used in passing from tonic to mediant.

The fourth scale degree is called the **subdominant,** because it lies five steps *below* the tonic. The subdominant also lies a half step above the mediant and has a strong tendency to move toward it. It may also be used in passing from mediant to dominant.

The sixth scale degree is called the **submediant,** as it lies halfway between tonic and subdominant. The submediant frequently acts as a neighbor to the dominant or in passing from dominant to upper tonic.

The seventh scale degree is called the **leading tone,** as it tends to lead into the tonic. This tendency is established by the half step between the two scale degrees.

# Music for Study

*You will recall from our earlier example of "Home, Sweet Home" that melodies move in a variety of ways. At times the melody moves by step from scale degree to scale degree. This motion is called* **scalar** *or* **conjunct.** *At other times the melody skips from one scale degree to another. This is called* **disjunct** *motion. In addition, pitches may be directly repeated. Melodies typically use all three types of motion.*

*Any scale is, strictly speaking, an abstraction. It represents a systematic arrangement of the pitch material that has been used in a piece of music. Much of the time, melodies use only fragments of scales, moving in either direction, but there are instances where complete scales appear. These melodies let us see, in a preliminary way, the way the music is organized and the parts the various scale degrees play.*

*"Joy to the World"*   GEORGE FREDERICK HANDEL (1685–1759)

*What is the key of this piece? Note all the occurrences of the tonic. Next, note the occurrences of dominant and mediant. Finally, consider how the other scale degrees are used in relationship to tonic, dominant, and mediant. Note particularly where the half steps of the scale occur.*
*Some of the factors that influence how we hear these relationships are:*

> *1. Metric placement—notes that fall on accented beats are generally felt to be structurally more significant.*

2. *Longer notes are also felt to be more important.*
3. *Pitches that* initiate *musical motions are often important, and certainly those pitches that* conclude *musical motions are important.*

*Here is another familiar Christmas carol:*

*"The First Noel"*   TRADITIONAL

*Again, notice how the melody is "anchored" by the tonic and dominant, with the mediant as a third point of reference.*

*Here are several other examples of predominantly scalar music:*

**EXAMPLE 1**

*Piano Trio, Op. 97*   LUDWIG VAN BEETHOVEN (1770–1827)

**EXAMPLE 2**

*"Caro Nome"* from *Rigoletto*    GIUSEPPE VERDI (1813–1901)

Translation: Dear name, which first made my heart throb, must always recall to me the delight of love!

**EXAMPLE 3**

*"The Easy Winners"*    SCOTT JOPLIN (1868–1917)

**EXAMPLE 4**

*"Everybody's Got a Home but Me"*

RICHARD RODGERS (1902–1979)    LYRICS BY OSCAR HAMMERSTEIN II (1895–1960)

*Example 4 continued*

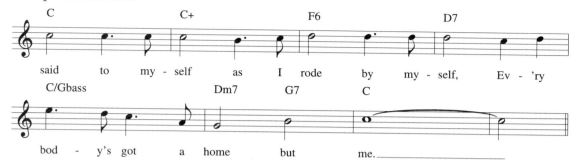

said    to    my - self    as    I    rode    by    my - self,    Ev - 'ry

bod - y's got    a    home    but    me._____

Lyrics by Oscar Hammerstein II. Music by Richard Rodgers. Copyright © 1955 by Richard Rodgers and Oscar Hammerstein II. Copyright Renewed. WILLIAMSON MUSIC owner of publication and allied rights throughout the world. International Copyright Secured. All Rights Reserved.

*Note in the following popular melody how the presence of the half steps establishes F as tonic of the scale, even though the pitch F is not heard prominently until the very end. Note also how the leap from D to E in the next-to-last measure actually completes the scale, but in a lower register.*

**EXAMPLE 5**

*"The Sound of Music"*

RICHARD RODGERS (1902–1979)    LYRICS BY OSCAR HAMMERSTEIN II (1895–1960)

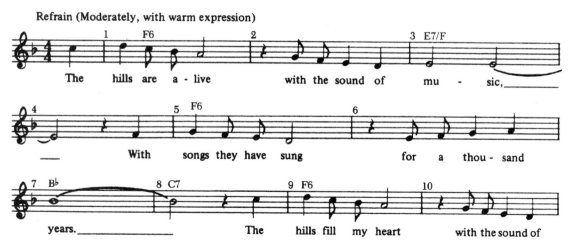

**Refrain (Moderately, with warm expression)**

The    hills    are a - live    with the sound of    mu - sic,_____

_____    With    songs they have    sung    for    a    thou - sand

years._____    The    hills fill    my    heart    with the sound of

*Example 5 continued*

*In Example 5, how do the arrival points on E in measures 3 and 11, and the arrival on B♭ in measure 7, contribute to the sense of forward motion in this melody? What is the effect of "withholding" tonic until the very end?\**

*From the preceding discussion, we might draw a few conclusions. The tonic, dominant, and mediant are frequently used as points of arrival or rest, and, in fact, we often call them* inactive *scale degrees. The other pitches tend to act as passing notes or neighboring notes, and we call these pitches* active *scale degrees. Like so much in music, these principles are by no means hard and fast, and we will see ample latitude in their application. Nonetheless, this is an important concept and one that is basic to understanding musical organization.*

---

\*Harmonic considerations are obviously very important in this melody but must await our full discussion of chords in Chapter 10.

# FIVE

# Compound Meter

## Suggested Listening

Franz von Suppé, *The Light Cavalry Overture,* second theme
(Allegretto Brillante)

Morton Gould, ***American Salute***

John Philip Sousa, *Washington Post March*

Nicolai Rimsky-Korsakov, ***Sheherazade,*** first movement
(from m. 18 on); third movement

Meredith Willson, "Seventy-six Trombones" from *The Music Man*

The characteristic lilt of these examples owes to the frequent use of a long-short rhythmic pattern. If we listen carefully, we will find that each beat is divided into three equal parts, and this is what defines a **compound meter.**

A compound meter presents several problems. We know from our earlier discussion that our basic note-value symbols are always divided into *two* of the next smallest value, and we can't divide a note into three parts using any of the standard note values.

There are two possible solutions to this dilemma. First, we can use what we call a **triplet** figure. This is a type of proportional notation that means to play three notes in the time of two. Stated as a ratio, it would be 3:2, but we simply use the 3, along with a slur or bracket for unbeamed notes:

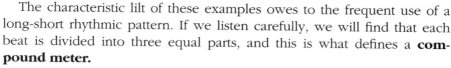

However, if an entire piece uses these divisions, the triplet becomes very cumbersome. The second possibility is to work up from the value of the division itself, what we call the **background unit.** If we need three background units for every beat, it follows that we can then sum these values into a single *dotted note,* and this value can then be used to represent the beat in compound meters:

(background)    ♪ ♪ ♪  =  ♩.  (beat unit)

(background)    ♩ ♩ ♩  =  ♩.  (beat unit)

But how do we express this organization in a meter signature? In a simple meter, we can designate the beat unit by a digit: 4 for ♩, 2 for ♩, and so on. But a dotted note would become a fractional number: ♩. = 4 1/2 (?). We could simply use the note value: $\frac{2}{\text{♩.}}$ or $\frac{3}{\text{♩.}}$. Unfortunately, this has not become standard usage.

Instead, we must represent the background unit in the meter signature. The upper number is then derived by counting the total number of background units:

♪ ♪ ♪   ♪ ♪ ♪  =  $\frac{6}{8}$
♩.        ♩.

The term *compound* implies that we feel subgroups of three rhythmic values, and there is an implied accent pattern within the subgroup:

$\frac{6}{4}$    ♩ ♩ ♩ ♩ ♩ ♩
       >  ⌣  ⌣  >  ⌣  ⌣

This is not unlike two measures of $\frac{3}{4}$, and the distinction between the two meters is not always clear. In fact, we often feel the pulse of compound meters at the level of the background unit and even count the music at that level, especially when the tempo is slow. Consider this example:

*"Silent Night"*    FRANZ GRÜBER (1787–1863)

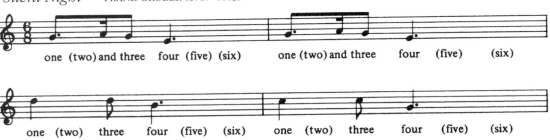

one (two) and three   four (five) (six)    one (two) and three   four (five) (six)

one (two)  three   four (five) (six)    one (two)  three   four (five) (six)

Compare:

A quicker example is more easily counted like this:

*"The Wild Horseman"*   ROBERT SCHUMANN (1810–1856)

The "trick" in counting rhythms is to keep simple and compound meters distinct. Certain patterns are difficult to distinguish clearly and must be counted with care, always mentally keeping the smallest value clear and steady. For example:

Keep the notes even in value!

Here is another. Count it the same way.

If you find the use of the same vocables for both simple and compound meters confusing, try using this traditional system for counting compound meter:

Like simple meters, compound meters are grouped according to the number of beats in each measure. **Compound duple** meters have two beats per measure, and for reasons explained earlier, the upper number of the time signature is always **6. Compound triple** meters have three beats per measure, and the upper number of the signature is always **9. Compound quadruple** meters have four beats per measure, and the upper number of the signature always is **12.** Any value can be designated as the background unit, and it is this value that is represented in the lower number of the signature.

$\frac{6}{4}$, $\frac{6}{8}$, $\frac{6}{16}$    are all compound duple meters;

$\frac{9}{4}$, $\frac{9}{8}$, $\frac{9}{16}$    are all compound triple; and

$\frac{12}{4}$, $\frac{12}{8}$, $\frac{12}{16}$    are all compound quadruple.

Conversely, you can always determine the number of beats in a compound meter signature by dividing the upper number by three.

Ties are also used in compound meters to express durations beyond those of the basic note values. However, since the dotted note is routinely used in compound meters to represent the value of the beat, in order to achieve rhythmic clarity and ease in reading, values that span even the beats themselves must use the tie.

This is incorrect!

In the case of compound triple meters, the only way the full value of a measure can be expressed is with a tied value.

And, as with simple meters, values spanning the barline must also use the tie.

## Computer Exercise

Chapter 5    Compound Meter
Compound Meters
1. Inserting Barlines—Compound Meters—All Levels    Drills #65–68
2. Completing Measures—Compound Meters—All Levels    Drills #69–72
3. Playing Practice—Compound Meters    Drills #73–84
Level 1—Values of 1 Beat or More
Level 2—Subdivisions
Level 3—Both

## Written Exercises

*Add barlines in the appropriate places. Place a double bar at the end of each example. The first note is always on a downbeat.*

# Music for Study: Counting Compound Meter

*As before, write out and count the rhythms of the following melodies. Identify
the meter of each. How many beats in a measure? What is the unit of the
beat? What is the background unit? See the Glossary for definitions of the
tempo terms. Does it seem more comfortable to count the beat unit, or the
background unit?*

*Here are a few of the most common patterns you will encounter. Count
each of them two ways: first, counting the beat unit, and second, counting
the background unit.*

## EXAMPLE 1

*"Sailing"*    TRADITIONAL

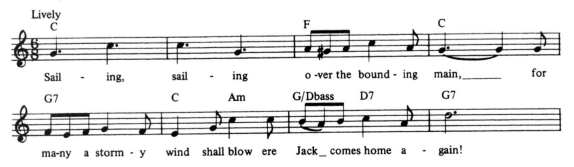

*Example 1 continued*

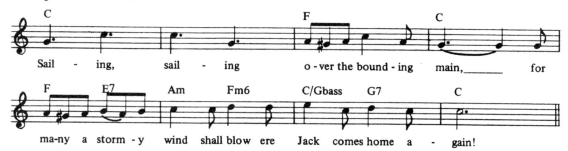

Sail — ing,    sail — ing    o - ver the bound - ing    main,_____    for

ma-ny    a storm - y    wind    shall blow ere    Jack    comes home    a - gain!

**EXAMPLE 2**

*"For He's a Jolly Good Fellow"*    ANONYMOUS

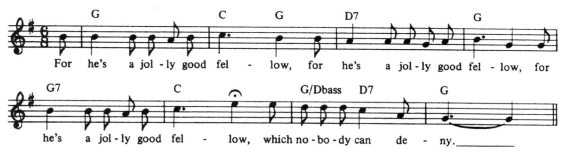

For    he's    a jol - ly good fel - low,    for    he's    a jol - ly good fel - low,    for

he's    a jol - ly good fel - low,    which no - bo - dy can    de - ny._____

**EXAMPLE 3**

*"When Johnny Comes Marching Home"*    TRADITIONAL

With spirit

1. When John-ny comes march-ing home a - gain, Hur - rah,____    hur - rah!____    We'll give him a heart - y

wel - come then, Hur - rah,____    hur - rah!___    The_ men will cheer,    the    boys    will shout,    The

la - dies, they_    will    all    turn out, And we'll all    feel    gay,    When    John-ny comes marching home.

**EXAMPLE 4**

*"Still wie die Nacht"*    KARL BOHM (1844–1920)

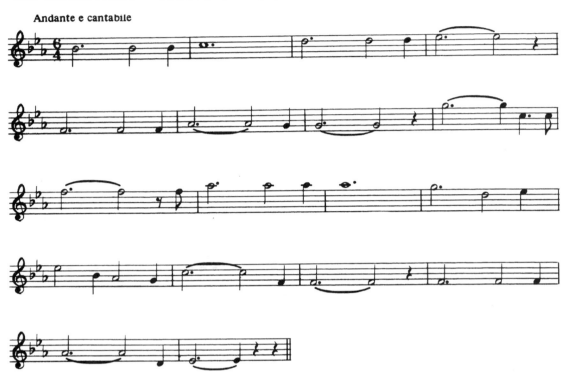

**EXAMPLE 5**

*Sonatina in G, Romanza*    LUDWIG VAN BEETHOVEN (1770–1827)

**EXAMPLE 6**

*Sheherazade*   NICOLAI RIMSKY-KORSAKOV (1844–1908)

**EXAMPLE 7**

*"Gypsy Love Song"*   VICTOR HERBERT (1859–1924)

**EXAMPLE 8**

*Nocturne Op. 9, No. 2*   FREDERICK CHOPIN (1810–1849)

## CLASSIFICATION OF METERS

In summary, meters are classified first as simple or compound, and then as to the number of beats per measure; meters having two beats per measure are called **duple,** those with three **triple,** and those with four **quadruple.** Meters with the same number of beats, but with a different division, have a strong relationship, and patterns common to one are often found in the other. A common example would be with the meters $\frac{2}{4}$ and $\frac{6}{8}$.

The same rhythmic pattern is notated above first in a simple duple meter and then in the equivalent compound meter. The **duplet** accomplishes in a compound meter what the triplet accomplishes in a simple meter.

The following excerpt illustrates the concept of equivalent meters very neatly. The first three measures are in compound quadruple meter with ♩. as the beat unit. In measure four, the meter changes to the equivalent *simple* quadruple meter with ♩ as the beat unit. The *tempo* of the beat stays the same, but instead of three notes per beat there are only two, making the eighth notes in effect longer and slower, as you can tell by listening to and counting this example. It's a simple yet very effective device.

*Symphony No. 5, Second Movement*    PETER TCHAIKOVSKY (1840–1893)

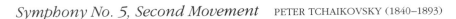

*Symphony No. 5, Second Movement continued*

**Changes to the equivalent simple meter ( ♩. = ♩ )**

All the common meters along with their classification will be found in the following table. Keep this page handy for reference.

## Table of Meter Signatures

| | SIMPLE | | | COMPOUND | | |
|---|---|---|---|---|---|---|
| | Meter | Beat Unit | Background Unit | Meter | Beat Unit | Background Unit |
| **DUPLE** | 2/2 ¢ | 𝅗𝅥 | ♩ | 6/4 | 𝅗𝅥. | ♩ |
| | 2/4 | ♩ | ♪ | 6/8 | ♩. | ♪ |
| | 2/8 | ♪ | ♬ | 6/16 | ♪. | ♬ |
| | 2/16 | ♬ | 𝅘𝅥𝅱 | | | |
| **TRIPLE** | 3/2 | 𝅗𝅥 | ♩ | 9/4 | 𝅗𝅥. | ♩ |
| | 3/4 | ♩ | ♪ | 9/8 | ♩. | ♪ |
| | 3/8 | ♪ | ♬ | 9/16 | ♪. | ♬ |
| | 3/16 | ♬ | 𝅘𝅥𝅱 | | | |
| **QUADRUPLE** | 4/2 | 𝅗𝅥 | ♩ | 12/4 | 𝅗𝅥. | ♩ |
| | 4/4 c | ♩ | ♪ | 12/8 | ♩. | ♪ |
| | 4/8 | ♪ | ♬ | 12/16 | ♪. | ♬ |
| | 4/16 | ♬ | ♬ | | | |

## Written Exercises

1. Write in the proper values as indicated for each meter: In the first measure, notate the beat units for each beat; in the second measure, notate the background units for each beat; and in the last measure, write in a single value (if possible) or tied values that represent the entire measure.

2. Complete the following measures. You may use a single note or several notes, as is appropriate.

3. Complete the last measure of each given example. Remember that the value of the upbeat is subtracted from the value of the final measure.

4. Examine each of the following rhythm patterns. Note whether the smaller values are grouped in twos (indicating a simple meter) or in threes (indicating a compound meter). Count the number of beats. Then, identify the meter of each example. Place the meter signature on the staff, in its appropriate place. In certain instances, there may be two possibilities, such as $\frac{2}{4}$ or $\frac{4}{8}$. Always reduce to one of the common meters listed in the Table of Meter Signatures (for example, reduce $\frac{8}{8}$ to $\frac{4}{4}$ or $\frac{2}{2}$).

a.

5. Complete the following chart:

| | Meter | Classification | Number of Beats | Beat Unit | Background Unit |
|---|---|---|---|---|---|
| | $\frac{4}{4}$ | simple quadruple | four | ♩ | ♪ |
| 1. | $\frac{9}{8}$ | | | | |
| 2. | $\frac{2}{4}$ | | | | |
| 3. | 𝄴 | | | | |
| 4. | $\frac{6}{4}$ | | | | |
| 5. | $\frac{3}{16}$ | | | | |
| 6. | $\frac{4}{8}$ | | | | |
| 7. | 𝄵 | | | | |
| 8. | $\frac{3}{4}$ | | | | |
| 9. | $\frac{4}{2}$ | | | | |
| 10. | $\frac{12}{16}$ | | | | |

# MORE ON THE USE OF BEAMS

As in simple meters, beams are used in a compound meter to group all flagged values that fall within a beat. The beats are always kept separate by the beams, and the number of notes within a beamed group will always be three or some multiple of three, thus reinforcing the basic character of the meter. For some examples, review the counting exercises on pages 78–81.

## Written Exercises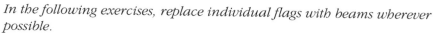

*In the following exercises, replace individual flags with beams wherever possible.*

Simple and compound groupings should be kept distinct; that is, smaller values should always be beamed in twos or multiples of two in a simple meter, and beamed in threes in a compound meter. In the example below, the same sequence of rhythmic values is beamed first in a compound meter and then in a simple meter. Count each example so that you can feel the implied accents.

Often, accent patterns in, say, $\frac{6}{8}$ and $\frac{3}{4}$ will be alternated or combined. This device is called **hemiola** and is characteristic of much Latin American music.

*"Guadalajara"*   PEPE GUIZAR

Recorded on "Mariachi Hits" (cassette only) CMP 1820.

*Concierto de Aranjuez*   JOAQUIN RODRIGO (1901– )

You can also hear the frequent use of hemiola in such pieces as "America" from Leonard Bernstein's *West Side Story* or Aaron Copland's *El Salón México*.

Another sort of hemiola can be created by tying values across the barline. This is a type of syncopation and is illustrated in Examples 3 and 4 on pages 144 and 145.

## Written Exercises

*In the following exercises, replace individual flags with beams wherever possible. Remember the meter signature!*

# ESTABLISHING METER THROUGH ACCENTS AND PATTERNS

## Music for Study

*Review the melodies used for the exercises in counting in Chapter 3 and earlier in this chapter. How is the meter of each melody established? On which counts do long notes occur? Short notes? Where the note values are uniform, what other devices seem to give a sense of the meter?*

It is somewhat misleading to look at a meter signature and then *see* how the meter is established. We must always bear in mind that music is intended to be *heard* and must be understood without necessary recourse to the notated score. How the composer accomplishes this little feat will be of some interest to us.

Music, unless a single unaccompanied line, is a composite of many rhythmic patterns, all unified and held together by a common beat unit. In Chapter 1, we described music as having **texture;** by this we meant the number of individual voices or parts and their mutual relationships. However different the rhythms of the various parts might be, they all will in some way serve to establish and reinforce the meter. In complex textures, one voice or part will nearly always clearly define the beat unit. This part is frequently the **bass line,** which is the lowest sounding part, and we generally listen for the beat in the bass instruments—string bass, tuba, etc.—or in the drum parts of a jazz or rock band, for example.

Establishment of meter involves both selection from among the possible note values and organization of the chosen durations so that the listener perceives the pulse or beat and can readily tell which beats are accented or stressed and which are not.

Accent or stress can be established in a number of ways. One way is by actually accenting a note by playing it louder or with a sharp attack. This type of accent is called a **dynamic accent.** Such attacks are indicated by accent marks placed over or under the noteheads: (These and other symbols were discussed in Chapter 1. The same thing can be accomplished by having more instruments play on a given beat or by using a relatively denser combination of pitches.

Another way to establish accent or stress is by varying durations. Everything being equal, a longer note will be felt to carry an accent. A pattern of durations such as will easily be perceived as a triple meter. An accent by duration is called an **agogic accent.**

Finally, *pattern* plays an important role in establishing meter. This is most obviously the case in accompanimental rhythms to music such as marches and dances.

Let's examine a specific musical example.

### *Triumphal March from* Peter and the Wolf

SERGE PROKOFIEV (1891–1953)

*Triumphal March continued*

Here is a rhythmic schematic of measures 5–12:

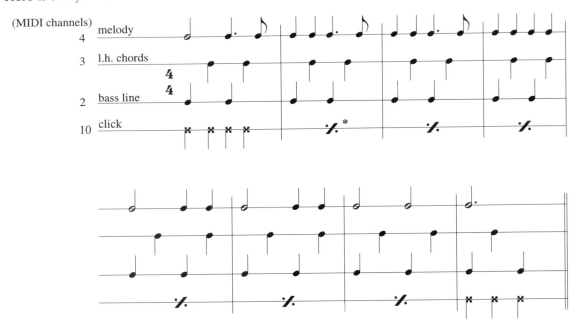

* `✕.` means repeat previous measure.

There are three easily distinguishable textural elements: (1) the melodic line, which is the highest voice in the right hand or treble staff; (2) the middle-register chords found in the bass clef on beats two and four; and (3) the bass line, the lowest notes in the left-hand part occurring on beats one and three. (See the rhythmic schematic.)

The melodic line uses both dynamic accents (as in measures 5, 6, 7, 9, 10, etc.) and agogic accents (as in measures 5, 9, and 10). The rhythmic patterns within each measure clearly support the meter and are frequently repeated from measure to measure.

As we would expect, the beat is clearly established in the bass line and the accompanimental left-hand chords, the bass line having the accented beats with the chords coming on the weak beats.

Waltzes and most other **genres** (types of compositions) having origins in dance music establish the meter in ways similar to the Prokofiev march. The bass line here marks the downbeat, and the chords come on the upbeats. The melody uses agogics and patterns that support the meter. Note again the repetitions and consequent limited variety of rhythms.

*Waltz in B-flat Major*    FRANZ SCHUBERT (1797–1828)

*Waltz in B-flat Major continued*

The next example is in compound meter. Note how the beat is established by the bass line, especially beginning in the fifth measure, where the bass line consists of a steady succession of dotted quarter notes—the beat unit. The division of the beat into three eighth notes is most clearly heard in the right hand of the piano accompaniment. With the metric organization thus so clearly established, the violin line is free to develop in a variety of rhythmic patterns.

*Sonata in D Major for Violin and Piano*    FRANZ SCHUBERT (1797–1828)

*Sonata in D Major for Violin and Piano continued*

## Exploring Rhythm and Meter at the Computer

*On your CD-ROM, you will find a folder labeled "MIDI files" containing MIDI sequences for the Prokofiev example and the two Schubert pieces above. You will also find MIDI sequences for the five examples that follow, laid out in the same format. These files can be accessed by your computer's multimedia software or a MIDI sequencer program. The various musical elements have been assigned to individual MIDI channels so that you can clearly hear how the establishment of the meter is built up. As a reference, a click track has been provided on channel ten. This is, in effect, a metronome corresponding to the beat unit. MIDI channel two contains the bass line, channel three contains the left-hand chords or figuration, and channel four contains the melodic elements. You can explore how meter is established by listening to the individual channels or by adding channels one by one.*

In the following instance, the bass marks the beat and the chords come "off the beat":

*The Thunderer March*    JOHN PHILIP SOUSA (1854–1932)

The melodic pattern of the bass notes themselves establishes the strong-weak differentiation.

There are many variations of this scheme. Here are two additional examples:

*March Militaire*    FRANZ SCHUBERT (1797–1828)

*The Stars and Stripes Forever (Trio)*    JOHN PHILIP SOUSA (1854–1932)

Melodic rhythms are more subtle but can also establish a metric pattern. Consider the following examples:

*Prelude*    JOHANN SEBASTIAN BACH (1685–1750)

*Sonata, Op. 2, No. 1, Third Movement*

LUDWIG VAN BEETHOVEN (1770–1827)

The repetition of a musical pattern at a different pitch level is called **sequence.** The basic pattern is typically repeated at successively higher or lower pitch levels, with from two to four repetitions. It is not unusual to find slight variations in the pitch pattern, as in the Beethoven example above. Or, intervals within the pattern may expand or contract, often with one note remaining stationary as a sort of anchor. And the pattern may be inverted, or turned upside-down. These last two devices are found in the Bach example above. What tends to remain constant is the rhythmic component.

## Written Exercises

*Listen to the following examples and then write out and analyze the rhythms of both  melody and accompaniment. What is the beat unit? Where is the beat most clearly established—melody or accompaniment? In which voice? Is the meter simple or compound? What characteristic rhythmic patterns occur? How are accented beats, particularly downbeats, established?*

**EXAMPLE 1**

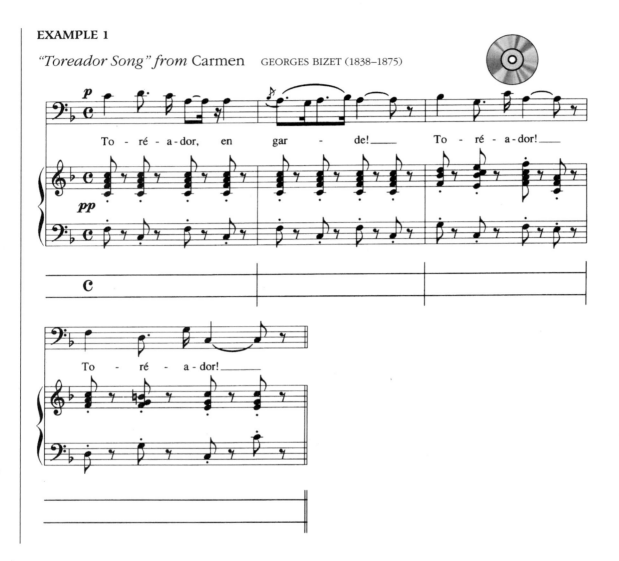

*"Toreador Song" from* Carmen    GEORGES BIZET (1838–1875)

**EXAMPLE 2**

*"Boil That Cabbage Down"*    TRADITIONAL

**EXAMPLE 3**

*"Knight Rupert"*   ROBERT SCHUMANN (1810–1856)

**EXAMPLE 4**

*"Venetian Boat Song"*   FELIX MENDELSSOHN (1809–1847)

*Example 4 continued*

**EXAMPLE 5**

*"Oh, What a Beautiful Mornin'"*

RICHARD RODGERS (1902–1979)    LYRICS BY OSCAR HAMMERSTEIN II (1895–1960)

*Example 5 continued*

feel - in' Ev - 'ry - thing's go - in' my way._____

## Computer Exercise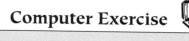

Chapter 5    Compound Meter
  4. Rhythmic Composition—Compound Meters    Drill #85

## Creating Rhythms at the Computer

*You will be given a meter signature with four empty bars and a limited number of rhythmic values from which to choose. When creating your rhythms, start with simple patterns that are coherent and clearly imply the meter (putting longer notes on metric accents, for example). Strive for movement across the barline. It is not necessary (or even desirable) to avoid repetition, but you should have some variety. End your patterns with longer notes, those of a full measure or at least a half measure in duration. The computer will then play back your patterns. If you have incomplete measures or measures with too many notes, the computer will prompt you to try again.*

# SIX

# The Minor Mode

## Suggested Listening

Franz Schubert, "Frülingssehnsucht" from *Schwanengesang,* mm. 13–30 (first verse); mm. 103–123 (fifth verse)

Johannes Brahms, "Vergebliches Ständchen," mm. 1–20 (first verse); mm. 43–60 (third verse)

Bedřich Smetana, *The Moldau,* mm. 40–49; mm. 333–350

Peter Tchaikovsky, Symphony No. 5, first movement, mm. 1–8; fourth movement, mm. 1–8, mm. 474–481

Cole Porter, "I Love Paris," refrain, mm. 1–16; mm. 17–36

Michel Legrand, Theme from *Summer of '42,* mm. 1–8; mm. 9–25

Discuss the difference in mood or character between the paired examples in each piece listed above.

Aside from some obvious differences in register, dynamics, and instrumentation, all of these examples illustrate the dramatic contrast of **mode.** We often associate mode changes with mood: Music in the major mode seems brighter and more cheerful, maybe even optimistic. The other commonly used mode—the minor mode—seems darker, more somber, even sad. The term mode, strictly defined, refers to the exact placement of half steps within the seven-tone scale. There are actually a number of modes, but for the time being we will be concerned with only two of them—major and minor.

The major mode is, of course, represented by the major scale. The minor mode is a bit more problematic, since there are three forms the scale may take.

Consider these well-known folk tunes. All have been written out in the same key (E minor) for ease of comparison.

**EXAMPLE 1**

*"God Rest Ye Merry, Gentlemen"*    TRADITIONAL

**EXAMPLE 2**

*"Que Ne Suis-Je La Fougère"*    TRADITIONAL FRENCH

**EXAMPLE 3**

*"Greensleeves"*   TRADITIONAL

We notice that the first five notes of each scale are uniform and have the pattern whole–half–whole–whole:

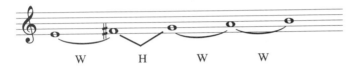

The remaining pitches in the first example yield the following scale:

This form of the minor scale is called **natural** or **pure minor.**

In the second example, we notice that the seventh scale degree has been consistently raised. This gives us the following scale form, called **harmonic minor:**

The harmonic minor still leaves a half step between degrees five and six, and there is a strong tendency for six to move to five (active to inactive, again). A "gap" is opened up between degrees six and seven. This largish-sounding interval is in fact called an **augmented second.**

In the third example, there is a variability in both the sixth and seventh scale degrees. At times they appear as they would in natural minor, but at other times one or both are raised. When both are raised, we have **melodic minor:**

The reasons for having this variety of minor scales are complex and involve traditions dating from the sixteenth century. But in general terms, we can understand these permutations in terms of the tendencies of the scale degrees.

You will recall from our discussion of the major scale the strong tendency of the leading tone to progress to tonic because of the half step active-to-inactive relationship. The natural minor lacks this half step. In fact, we often call the seventh degree in natural minor the **subtonic.** This lack of a leading tone somewhat affects the centric attraction of the tonic, and melodies in natural minor must be carefully structured to establish the tonic in other ways. The harmonic minor scale furnishes a true leading tone by the simple device of chromatically raising the seventh scale degree. We will see later that there are important harmonic (chordal) associations with this alteration. Now, if one wishes to pass smoothly from dominant up to tonic, the gap can be troublesome. To bridge this gap, the sixth degree is also raised, giving rise to melodic minor. Traditionally, when the music is descending from tonic to dominant, the scale reverts to its *natural* form. Accordingly, we write melodic minor both ascending and descending:

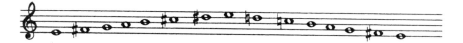

In actual practice, the ascending form will appear in passages moving in either direction, but this is because of harmonic considerations.

## USE OF ACCIDENTALS IN THE MINOR MODE

The various alterations of scale degrees six and seven are not indicated by the key signature but must be indicated by an accidental each time the note appears. If a note is otherwise unaltered by the key signature, that note is raised by a sharp:

If that note is already raised by the key signature, a double sharp is called for:

If a note is flatted by the key signature, the note is raised by a natural sign:

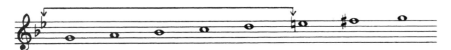

The rule is that a single accidental will apply to every note in the *same register* throughout a given measure. Notes in other registers must have their own accidentals. A barline cancels the accidental, but parenthetical or cautionary accidentals are often used anyway:

## Computer Exercise

Chapter 6    The Minor Mode
Minor Scale Forms

1. Minor Scale Writing—All Levels    Drills #86–93
2. Minor Scale Spelling—All Levels    Drills #94–101
3. Minor Scale Recognition    Drill #102

## Written Exercises

*As before, when you feel you have mastered the computer drills, work out the following written exercises. Your instructor may ask you to hand in these exercises for purposes of evaluation.*

1. Add accidentals as required to make the following scales *natural minor:*

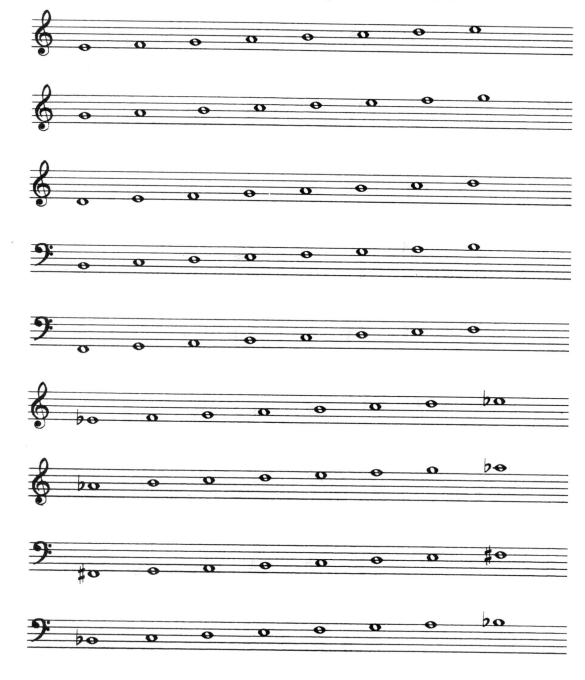

2. Make the following minor scales *harmonic* by adding the necessary accidental:

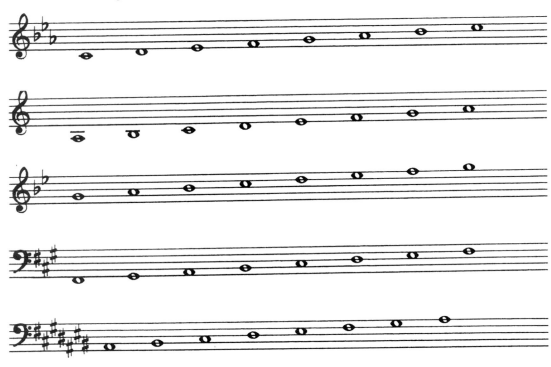

3. Make the following minor scales *melodic* by adding the necessary accidentals:

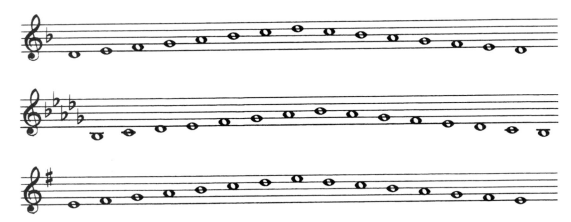

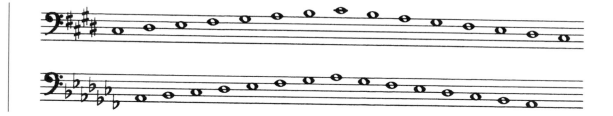

## INTERVALS IN THE MINOR MODE

Here are the seconds and thirds found in the various minor scales. Compare them with those found in the major scale. It is the difference in these intervals that gives the minor mode its unique "flavor."

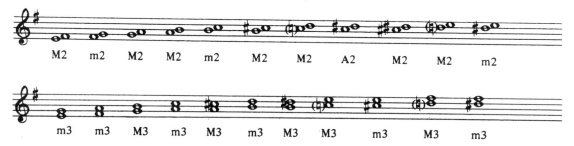

## RELATIVE AND PARALLEL MINORS

Every major key has both a relative and a parallel minor. (This relationship works both ways, of course. Every minor key has both a relative and parallel major.)

If we start on the sixth scale degree of any major scale and build a complete scale, we arrive at a natural minor scale that we call the **relative minor.** It follows that any major scale and its relative minor will share the same pitches and consequently the same key signature:

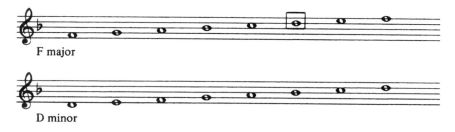

F major

D minor

Accordingly, every key signature will represent both a major key and a minor key. The following chart shows the circle of fifths with both modes for each key signature. Note: On this chart, and elsewhere in this book, capital letters represent major keys and lowercase letters represent minor keys.

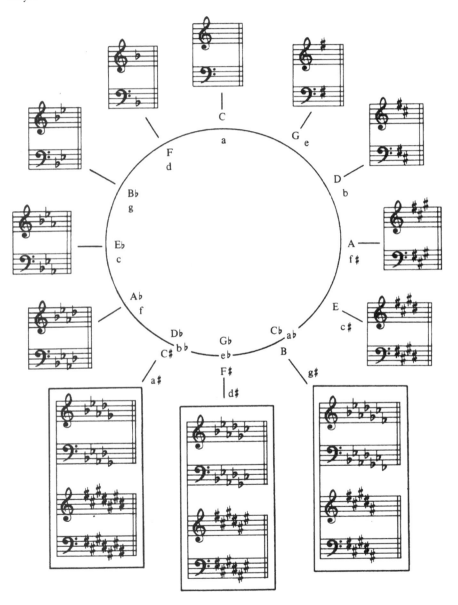

**Parallel modes** are those that share the same tonic. Examples are C major and C minor, A major and A minor, E♭ major and E♭ minor, and so on. Parallel modes obviously have different key signatures, and, in fact, there is a consistent difference of three accidentals between parallel modes.

F:          f:          E:          e:          D:          d:

A comparison of parallel modes indicates certain common pitches. We often call the tonic, dominant, and subdominant *tonal degrees,* since they are the same in parallel modes. The other scale degrees are called *modal degrees,* since they vary from mode to mode. In tonal music, the supertonic is also the same in parallel modes, and in fact this scale degree might well be considered a tonal degree. But as we will see in the next chapter, one of the so-called church modes—the Phrygian—is characterized by a lowered second scale degree, and so for the sake of simplicity we continue to refer to the supertonic as a modal degree. Of particular importance in major and minor tonal music are the mediant and the submediant, since these two scale degrees, more than any others, clearly establish the sense of mode. What common scalar patterns exist among the various scale forms?

## Computer Exercise

Chapter 6    The Minor Mode
Minor Key Signatures

1. Minor Key Signature Spelling—All Levels    Drills #103–104
2. Minor Key Signature Recognition—All Levels    Drills #105–106
3. Key Signature Recognition (Major & Minor)—All Levels    Drills #107–108

# Written Exercises

1. Name the *relative* key of each given key. Write out the key signatures
   and tonics of both keys, using both clefs of the great staff.
   *Example:* Given key: F major        Relative: D minor

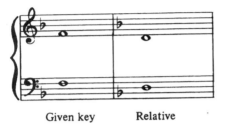

Given key        Relative

a. D major

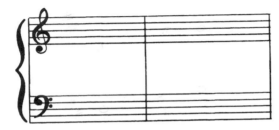

b. C minor

c. A♭ major

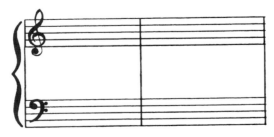

d.  F# minor

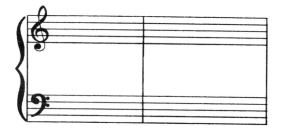

e.  G major

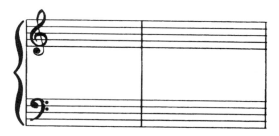

2. Name the *parallel* key of each given key. Write out the key signature
   and tonic note of both keys, using both clefs of the great staff.
   *Example:* Given key: G major      Parallel: G minor

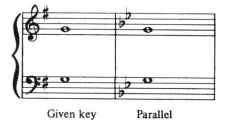

Given key      Parallel

a.  B♭ major

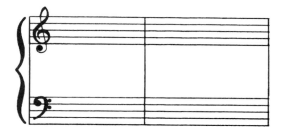

b. E♭ minor

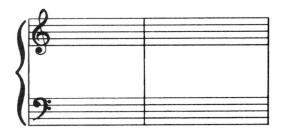

c. A major

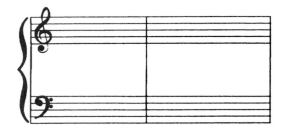

d. C♯ major

e. B minor

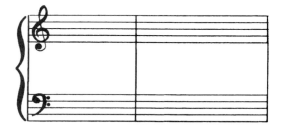

## Music for Study

*Look and listen to the following examples. Which note seems to be the tonic?*
*What scale degrees seem most clearly to establish the mode? What scale forms*
*are used? Does the scale remain constant throughout an example, or does*
*it change?*

### EXAMPLE 1

*"O Charlie Is My Darling"*    SCOTCH SONG

### EXAMPLE 2

*Trio*    FRANZ JOSEF HAYDN (1732–1809)

**EXAMPLE 3**

*Symphony No. 4, Second Movement*    PETER TCHAIKOVSKY (1840–1893)

**EXAMPLE 4**

*"First Loss"*    ROBERT SCHUMANN (1810–1856)

**EXAMPLE 5**

*"Ecossaise"*   FRANZ SCHUBERT (1797–1828)

**EXAMPLE 6**

*Hungarian Dance No. 5*   JOHANNES BRAHMS (1833–1897)

**EXAMPLE 7**

*"I Wonder as I Wander"*   APPALACHIAN CAROL

**EXAMPLE 8**

*Love Theme from* The Godfather   NINO ROTA (1911–1974)

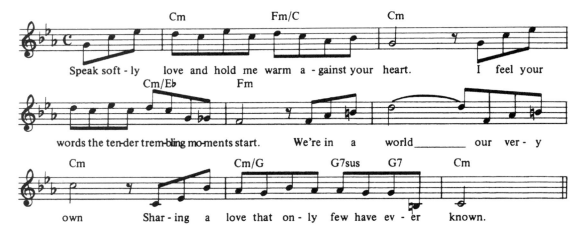

Words by Larry Kusik. Music by Nino Rota. Copyright © 1972 by Famous Music Corporation. International Copyright Secured. All Rights Reserved.

**EXAMPLE 9**

*"Danube Waves"*   ION IVANOVICI (1845–1902)

One can't always rely on the key signature (or lack of one) alone when determining the key and mode of a piece. Consider this melody by Haydn:

What is the tonic pitch of this melody? How is that pitch established as tonic? What scale degree is being raised by the sharp? What then is the scale being used?

Very often, a key signature will indicate only the overall key of an extended piece. The composer may change keys during the course of the movement and indicate the new key with accidentals only. Regardless, remember that we are aware of the key signature itself only when we are looking *at* the music, not when we are listening *to* it. But we certainly do hear tonic and the particular scale being used, and it's this that tells us what key and mode we are in!

In summary, look for tonic and dominant to be established by position and frequency—at the beginning or at the end of the music, or on metric accents. In minor, look for the presence of accidentals on the seventh, and also on the sixth, scale degrees. Remember that these scale degrees are variable.

# THE CHROMATIC SCALE

None of the scales discussed so far has consisted of more than seven different letter-named pitches. It is quite possible (and quite common) to compose simple pieces using only the notes of a given scale. We term such music **diatonic.**

Yet we know from our discussion of the keyboard and accidentals that other notes are also available. These other pitches are commonly introduced as decorative pitches or for "color" and, in fact, are called **chromatic** pitches, from the Greek word *chromos,* which means color.

The most frequent embellishments using chromatically altered pitches are neighbor tones and passing tones. Here are some examples:

Chromatic passing tones are naturally used to fill in the "space" between two notes a whole step apart. If we take a major or minor scale and fill in *all* the whole steps with chromatic half steps, we then have a **chromatic scale.** Note that the diatonic half steps remain constant. Enharmonic notes are also commonly substituted for double flat and double sharp notes.

Though sharps or naturals are normally used ascending and flats or naturals descending, the raised fourth degree is routinely used in both ascending and descending scales (see N.B. below). Similarly, a lowered sixth scale degree is often substituted for a raised fifth. In minor, both altered and unaltered seventh degrees must be considered diatonic.

N.B.    N.B.

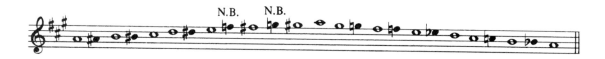

## Written Exercises

1.  Add notes to make the following scales chromatic:

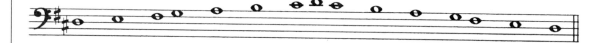

2.  Write chromatic scales, ascending and descending, starting on the given pitches:

## Music for Study

*What are the key and mode of the following examples? Which pitches are diatonic? Which chromatic? Are the chromatic pitches neighbors or passing tones?*

*Remember that an accidental not in the key signature applies to every note in the measure on the same line or space. (The same note in another register would need its own accidental.) A barline cancels the accidental.*

**EXAMPLE 1**

*Waltz in C Major*   FRANZ SCHUBERT (1797–1828)

**EXAMPLE 2**

*Jarabe Tapatio*   TRADITIONAL

**EXAMPLE 3**

*"Wonderful Copenhagen"*    FRANK LOESSER (1910–1969)

**EXAMPLE 4**

*"Barnum and Bailey's Favorite" (Trio)*    KARL L. KING (1891–1971)

**EXAMPLE 5**

*"Habanera" from* Carmen    GEORGES BIZET (1838–1875)

---

*Translation:* Love is a wild bird that none may tame, and one calls in vain . . .

**EXAMPLE 6**

*"Prelude to a Kiss"*   EDWARD "DUKE" ELLINGTON (1889–1972)

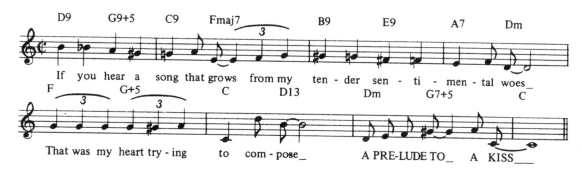

If you hear a song that grows from my ten - der sen - ti - men - tal woes_

That was my heart try - ing to com - pose_ A PRE-LUDE TO_ A KISS___

# SEVEN

# Other Scales

In Chapter 4, we stated that scales are merely abstractions; they are a convenient way of looking at the particular characteristics of the material of a given piece. We have devoted a lot of time to the major scale and the various minor scales because these are the scales that were used in the time period from roughly 1700 through 1900—from the baroque period, through the classical period, to the romantic period. In fact, these scales continue to be very much in use today, particularly in popular music.

## MODES

There are a number of other scales that should be mentioned, since they are used in the music of the Middle Ages (c. 1200–1450) and the Renaissance (c. 1450–1600), and also occur in folk music and contemporary music.

The modes, sometimes called the **church modes,** are very old. They form the basis for most music composed prior to 1600 and have been "stored away," so to speak, in the chants of the Roman Catholic Church. The modes enjoyed a resurgence of interest in the early part of this century and appear even in popular music and jazz.

We mentioned the use of the word **mode** in regard to the location of the half steps. In this sense, the modes are merely a series of scales having slightly different arrangements of whole and half steps. We can easily visualize the modes by thinking of the white keys of the piano. If we start on each pitch in turn we get all the modes.

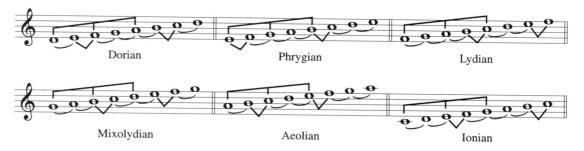

Dorian          Phrygian          Lydian

Mixolydian          Aeolian          Ionian

You have probably noticed that the white-key Ionian mode is the same as C major and that Aeolian is the same as A natural minor. Since these two modes first appeared in treatises at about the same time as the emergence of the major-minor system, historical purists tend not to count them among the church modes. There is also a white-key mode built on B called Locrian, but because of its inherent tonal instability it is rarely used.

Any mode can be written on any pitch, of course, simply by using accidentals or the appropriate key signature. Here are examples of modes transposed to other pitches:

G Dorian          E Mixolydian          D Phrygian

The modes are named after provinces of ancient Greece. This is handy nomenclature but has no other significance. Dorian, Phrygian, and Aeolian are called minor modes because of the minor third (step and a half) from tonic to mediant. Lydian, Mixolydian, and Ionian are major modes because of the major third (two steps) between tonic and mediant.

Modal music is *centric,* meaning that the tonic (or *final*) of the mode acts as a key center, just as in major and minor.

Here are some examples of modal music. Note how the characteristic intervals of whole step–half step patterns are emphasized. Identify the mode of each example.

## EXAMPLE 1

*"Scarborough Fair"*    TRADITIONAL

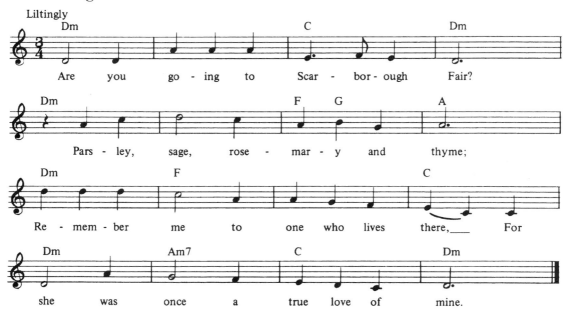

## EXAMPLE 2

*"Old Joe Clarke"*    TENNESSEE FOLKSONG

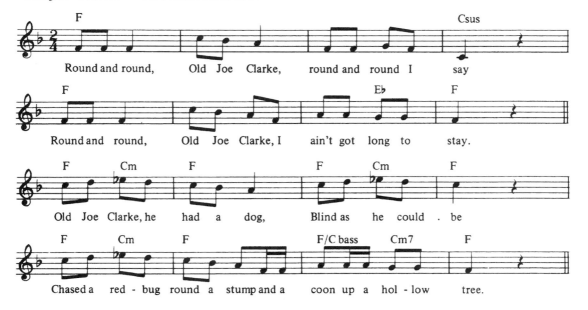

**EXAMPLE 3**

*Theme from* Hawaii Five-O     MORT STEVENS (1929–1991)

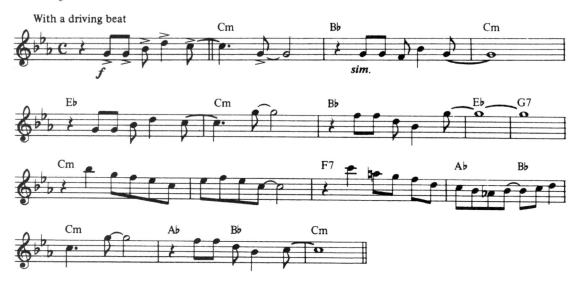

The use of A♮ in measure 12 has the effect of momentarily changing the mode. What is the mode in that measure? The appearance of A♭ in the following measure restores the original mode. This is another very common device in modal music.

*Hawaii Five-O* was a popular TV police drama during the '60s. It can still be seen in reruns. The theme song is available on the CD *CBS: The First 50 Years, Original TV Soundtracks,* TVT 1550.

**EXAMPLE 4**

*Theme from* The X-Files   MARK SNOW (1946–  )

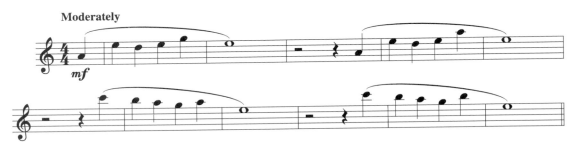

So pervasive is the traditional major and minor tonal system—even in contemporary popular music—that the simple use of a mode, along with some synthesized sounds, can create an effect that is, well, alien.

The X-files theme is available on the CD *Ultimate TV Drama Themes,* Dominion 4221.

## Suggested Listening

*Contemporary composers of popular music have frequently used the modes to good effect. But rather than writing whole tunes in a single mode, these composers mix modes, going back and forth from the modes to conventional major and minor.*

*The Beatles were a rock group that enjoyed a phenomenal success during the '60s and have enjoyed a revival in the '90s. Much of their music has a modal flavor, derived in part from their common British folk-music tradition and from the "rhythm and blues" idioms of '50s American rock and roll (Bill Haley, Elvis Presley, et al.).*

*The use of the flatted seventh degree in the major mode yields the Mixolydian mode. You can clearly hear this mode in the tune "Ticket to Ride" and many others. Typically, the mode won't be used throughout the tune, but will alternate with other modes or the regular major and minor scales.*

*"Norwegian Wood" illustrates the use of contrasting modes. The first four measures are in G Mixolydian (by virtue of the lowered seventh degree), whereas the second four measures are in G Dorian (characterized by the*

*progression from the G-minor chord to the C-major chord, which implies a G Dorian scale). The last four measures return to Mixolydian. The use of the F♯ suggests a momentary traditional G major.*

*"Can't Buy Me Love" is largely in Aeolian. The lovely "Eleanor Rigby" achieves its haunting effect through a mixture of Dorian and Aeolian. This is very sophisticated music! (All the Beatles' music is found in the complete CD boxed set Apple CDP 797036-2 and 797039-2.)*

*The opening phrase of "Walk On By," by Burt Bacharach and Hal David, has a pronounced Dorian flavor:*\*

*As the key signature suggests, the music progresses ultimately toward F major. You will find the last part of the tune on page 148.*

*The use of the raised fourth degree in major gives the melody the piquancy of the Lydian mode. Richard Rodgers uses this device in the opening phrase of "March of the Siamese Children," perhaps to suggest the exotic atmosphere of the East.*

*The Lydian mode also colors two of the most popular songs from Leonard Bernstein's* West Side Story, *"Maria" and "Tonight."*

---

\*The original version of "Walk On By" can be found on the CD *All Time Greatest Hits,* by Dionne Warwick, Rhino CD 71100.

One style of contemporary music that has much in common with modal music is the music we call "the blues." The blues takes its character from the use of the so-called blue notes—scale degrees that are inflected; these notes occur in both their raised and lowered forms, sometimes simultaneously. The end result is a scale that combines the characteristics of several modes and which may be thought of as a sort of "super mode." The most common blue notes are the third and seventh scale degrees. The fifth degree is also sometimes flatted, and the fourth degree is sometimes raised. These two enharmonic notes are somewhat interchangeable. You can hear the use of the "blues scale" in a wide range of popular music and jazz, from the compositions of W. C. Handy (1873–1958) to Elvis Presley's '50s hit song "Heartbreak Hotel," to a tune such as "A Call for All Demons" by the avant-garde jazz composer Sun Ra. The blues also has a very characteristic form, which is illustrated in Appendix 1.

## PENTATONIC SCALE

Still another scale is the pentatonic scale, which, as the name suggests, is a five-note scale. We know it most commonly as the scale formed by the black keys on the piano (in fact, a lot of pentatonic music uses only the black keys), and we tend (incorrectly) to associate it exclusively with the music of Asian countries. Like the modes, pentatonic scales can be written on any pitch. Here is the black-key scale and two other examples:

Pentatonic music is centric and generally very simple. Much folk music is pentatonic. Here are some examples:

**EXAMPLE 1**

*"Old Paint"*  TRADITIONAL

Good - by, old Paint, I'm a - leav - in' Chey - enne, Good - by, old

Paint, I'm a - leav - in' Chey - enne. I'm leav - in' Chey - enne, I'm off to Mon-

Scale:

tan - a, Good - by, old Paint, I'm a - leav - in' Chey - enne.

**EXAMPLE 2**

*"Hush My Babe"*  TRADITIONAL AMERICAN

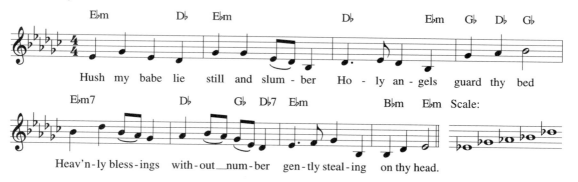

Hush my babe lie still and slum - ber Ho - ly an - gels guard thy bed

Heav'n - ly bless - ings with - out num - ber gen - tly steal - ing on thy head.

**EXAMPLE 3**

*"Pagodes"*    CLAUDE DEBUSSY (1862–1918)

Additional information on other kinds of scales and their use in music of other cultures will be found in Chapter 13.

## Computer Exercise

Chapter 7    Other Scales
   1. Other Scales    Drill #109

## Exploring Other Scales at the Computer

*Drill #109 gives you the opportunity to listen to the sounds of several of the scales presented in this chapter. Compare the sounds of these scales to those of the major and minor scales.*

# EIGHT

# More on Rhythm and Meter

## SYNCOPATION

Review the section "Establishing Meter Through Accents and Patterns" on pages 92–98, and then listen to this famous Scott Joplin rag.

*"The Easy Winners"*   SCOTT JOPLIN (1868–1917)

*"The Easy Winners" continued*

## Exploring Syncopation at the Computer

*The Scott Joplin rag is included in the MIDI files folder on your disk. MIDI channel ten contains a click track, channel two contains the bass line, channel three contains the left-hand chords, and channel four contains the melodic line. The effect of the syncopation can be experienced by playing the accompaniment first and then putting the melodic line against it. You might also want to play just the melody and the click track together.*

Notice how many instances there are of longer notes coming on weak beats and weak parts of beats. Agogic or dynamic accents that disagree with the meter are called **syncopations.** Syncopations are used for variety, but will be effective only if the metric organization is clearly established. Typically, a composer will start with regular rhythms and then use syncopations for effect. Or, as in the Joplin rag, syncopated melodic rhythms are used against regular accompanimental rhythms. Here are other examples:

**EXAMPLE 1**

*March in D Major*   JOHANN SEBASTIAN BACH (1685–1750)

**EXAMPLE 2**

*Italian Folksong*   PETER TCHAIKOVSKY (1840–1893)

*Example 2 continued*

**EXAMPLE 3**

*"Sobre Las Olas"*    JUVENTINO ROSAS (1868–1894)

**EXAMPLE 4**

*On the Beautiful Danube, Waltzes, Op. 314, No. 3*

JOHANN STRAUSS (1825–1899)

Examples 3 and 4 illustrate another typical sort of hemiola. You will recall from the discussion of compound meter that there is often a blurring of the distinction between simple triple and compound duple meter. The tempo of waltzes, in particular, allows one to feel the pulse as one-to-the-bar, much like a beat of compound meter. In this event, composers can create the hemiola effect by tying the third beat of one measure into the first beat of the next measure, creating the effect of a large measure of $\frac{3}{2}$ superposed over the $\frac{3}{4}$ of the accompaniment.

**EXAMPLE 5**

*"I Got Rhythm"*   GEORGE GERSHWIN (1898–1937)

Syncopation can also be affected by dynamic accents:

*Symphony No. 104, Third Movement*   FRANZ JOSEF HAYDN (1732–1809)

And syncopation can even result from melodic patterning:

*Symphony No. 5, Fourth Movement*    LUDWIG VAN BEETHOVEN (1770–1827)

In this example, Beethoven has created an implied accent by the leap from the first to the second eighth note in the first measure. This pattern is then repeated in the second measure. In the third measure, the syncopated pattern is used in both halves of the measure. Beethoven reinforces the effect of syncopation both by the use of articulations (the slur and staccato dots) and by the *sf* dynamic accent. These devices also serve to create the same sense of syncopated accent in the last half of measures 1 and 2 even though the leap does not occur here. Note that Beethoven indicates the start of the pattern by breaking the beam between the first and second eighth notes.

One very effective and common device for creating syncopation through patterning is to devise a musical motive or figure having an odd number of notes or a number that doesn't coincide with the normal organization of the meter. The rhythmic pattern is then "superimposed" on the regular meter, creating a rhythmic disjunction or rhythmic "dissonance." Here are some examples:

*"Fascinatin' Rhythm"*    GEORGE GERSHWIN (1898–1937)

*"In the Mood"*    JOE GARLAND (1903–1977)

Here is an example that combines agogic and dynamic accents along with a syncopated pattern in the accompaniment:

*"Walk On By"*    BURT BACHARACH (1929– )

Syncopated patterns are often notated with irregular beaming. Since the first of any beamed group suggests an accent, syncopations are created by beaming "against" the meter.

That is why it is important not to beam randomly!

## Computer Exercise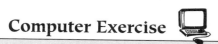

Chapter 8    More on Rhythm and Meter
1. Syncopation—Simple Meters    Drills #110–113
2. Syncopation—Compound Meters    Drills #114–117

# RHYTHM IN JAZZ AND POPULAR MUSIC

The unique character of contemporary jazz and the popular music from the 1920s up to our present day derives significantly from their rhythms. Syncopation, in particular, was eagerly adopted by composers of popular music and is found in some form in most popular music written in this century.

One of the more vexing issues in music history involves discrepancies between the way music is notated and the manner in which it is performed. Nowhere is this more evident than in jazz. Perhaps this is because jazz began as—and continues to be—a largely *improvised* art form, but it also has to do with the fundamental metric organization of the music—what we call its rhythmic "feel." The notation of jazz music nearly always comes after its creation and necessitates a certain number of notational compromises.

Ragtime music, as illustrated by the Joplin rag at the beginning of the chapter, was derived from march music as well as the two-step dances and waltzes of the time. All were characterized by the regular division of the beat into equal parts—what would come to be called "square" rhythms—and what we have defined as simple meter. At first the early Dixieland music that arose in New Orleans maintained this regular division, but at some point, as Dixieland music migrated north, the performers adopted the more lilting feel of the long-short rhythms. This created a rhythmic feeling quite similar to compound meter and its characteristic triple division of the beat. This new style, which came to be known as *swing,* became the dominant trend from the late '20s to the late '40s, though the even eighth-note feeling continued to be found in a genre called "eight-to-the-bar."

Jazz musicians often talk about "swinging the eighth notes." This means playing a written duple division of the beat as if it were long-short, or a compound division. Look again at the excerpt from "In the Mood" on page 147. Even though the music is written in a simple meter, with quarter notes divided into two eighth notes, it would be performed more like this:

Why it wasn't notated this way is one of those curious anomalies of music history. Perhaps it was because the simple-meter notation is, well, *simpler.*

Another genre of music that clearly uses the compound feel is the Delta blues. This music has its roots in the Deep South, particularly in Mississippi, where it remains a vital idiom to this very day. As you listen to this music, particularly the slow blues, you can hear very clearly the rolling triplets in the background.

During the '50s, American popular music was dominated by rhythm and blues, a term suggesting its obvious roots. A good illustration is the song "Heartbreak Hotel." This style of music used swing rhythms, but during the late '50s and early '60s there occurred another of those unaccounted-for changes, and seemingly overnight performers reverted to the even-eighths mode. This style soon became predominant and remains pretty much so to this day. Jazz music has now also begun to explore rock idioms, particularly the straight, or even, eighth-note rhythms. At the same time, in both jazz and pop music, those styles that derived from swing and the blues continue on, with performing groups using whichever style suits their particular song.

# Music for Study

*Listen to the recordings of these two contrasting examples of contemporary popular music. Pay particular attention to the bass and drums. Do you hear even divisions of the beat, or uneven divisions?*

*"Hey Jude"*   JOHN LENNON (1940–1980) AND PAUL MCCARTNEY (1942– )

Words and Music by John Lennon and Paul McCartney. Copyright © 1988 Sony/ATV Songs LLC. Copyright Renewed.
All Rights Administered by Sony/ATV Music Publishing, 8 Music Square West, Nashville, TN 37203. International
Copyright Secured. All Rights Reserved.

*"Sir Duke"*   STEVIE WONDER (1950– )

*"Sir Duke" continued*

Words and Music by Stevie Wonder. © 1978 JOBETE MUSIC CO., INC. and BLACK BULL MUSIC c/o EMI APRIL MUSIC INC. All Rights Reserved. International Copyright Secured. Used by Permission.

*Both of these examples use syncopations at the subdivision level. ("Hey Jude" actually uses syncopations at both the eighth-note and sixteenth-note level.) The difference in the sound of the sixteenth notes between the two examples is quite striking, even though both are notated in simple quadruple meter. John Lennon, Paul McCartney, and Stevie Wonder were all influenced by the rhythm and blues music of the '50s, but Wonder shows his indebtedness to jazz music as well. The excerpt from "Sir Duke" is a unison instrumental "break" that incorporates traditional jazz* **riffs.** *The use of the sixteenth notes creates a* double-time *effect, with the sixteenth notes "swung."*

*"Hey Jude" can be found on Apple CDP 797039-2. The original recording of "Sir Duke" by Stevie Wonder can be found on the CD set* Songs in the Key of Life, *Motown CD 3746303402.*

As you listen to jazz and popular music, pay particular attention to the background rhythms. Do you hear even eighth notes, or do you hear the triplets? An especially good example illustrating both styles can be heard on the song "I Want You (She's So Heavy)" from the Beatles' *Abbey Road* album. This song has a largely instrumental refrain that is slow-blues–based, and you can easily hear the rolling eighth-note triplets. The verse, by contrast, uses the straight, or even, eighth notes, and the two styles simply alternate as the song progresses. Interestingly enough, the sheet music to this song uses $\frac{12}{8}$ as a meter signature for the refrain and common time for the verse.

Additional information on rhythm and the rhythmic character of various folk cultures will be found in Chapter 13.

# NINE

# Intervals

We must now consider the topic of intervals in greater depth. You will recall that any two pitches, considered in their relationship one to another, form what we call an *interval*. If the notes are played in succession, we have a **melodic interval;** if played together, a **harmonic interval.**

*Melodic Intervals*

*Harmonic Intervals\**

As you will recall, the interval's name or classification gives us two important items of information: (1) the *size* of the interval, which is the number of scale degrees from one note to the other; and (2) *quality,* which refers to the exact number of semitones contained in the interval.

The size of intervals is a general property and unproblematic. A note in relation to itself (the same letter-name in the same register) is a **unison** or **prime,** and is indicated by the number 1. Two notes a degree apart form

---

\*Observe the way the unison and second are notated when written as harmonic intervals (asterisked intervals).

a *second* (indicated by the number 2), notes three degrees distant form a *third* (indicated by a 3), and so on.

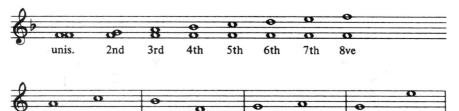

Quality is the more specific property that distinguishes intervals of notes with the same letter-names and thus the same *size*.

## SECONDS

We have already talked considerably about seconds. The half step is, in precise terms, a *minor second* (abbreviated m2). Minor in this sense means the small second. The whole step is a *major second* (abbreviated M2), major here meaning the large second. And we know there is a half-step difference between the two. We have also seen one instance of an *augmented second* (abbreviated A2), consisting of a step and a half. The augmented second is a half step larger than the major second. Let's compare all three:

Note that all three are considered to be seconds so long as the letter-names of the pitches are a degree apart. But the *quality* depends on the exact distance from one note to the other calculated in half steps.

## Exercises

*Review the computer drills on whole steps and half steps, as well as the written exercises for whole steps and half steps, from Chapter 4.*

# THIRDS

Because of the frequent occurrence of thirds in melodies, as well as their importance as the building blocks of chord structures, we should be very familiar with their qualities.

To review, the major third consists of two whole steps, and the minor third consists of a step and a half.

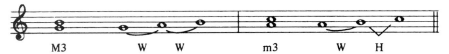

In our discussion of seconds, we mentioned the augmented second. We can also create an *augmented third,* by either raising the upper note or lowering the lower note of any major third.

There is one other quality of third, and that is *diminished.* We create this quality by reducing a *minor third,* by lowering the upper note or raising the lower note.

Seconds may also be diminished. The resultant sound is enharmonically a unison. This written interval is rare.

## Computer Exercise

Chapter 9    Intervals

1. Interval Writing—Level 1—Seconds & Thirds Only    Drills #118–119
2. Interval Spelling—Level 1—Seconds & Thirds Only    Drills #126–127
3. Interval Recognition—Level 1—Seconds & Thirds Only    Drill #134

## Written Exercises

1. Write major thirds *above* the given notes.

2. Write minor thirds *above* the given notes.

3. Write major thirds *below* the given notes.

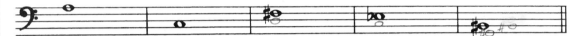

4. Write minor thirds *below* the given notes.

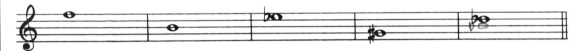

# THE PERFECT INTERVALS

Unisons, fourths, fifths, and octaves are special cases. Why this is so can be seen if we compare the intervals formed by each degree of a major and natural minor scale with tonic:

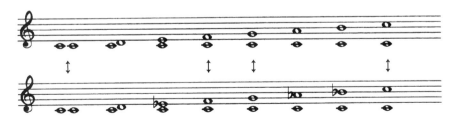

We see that the intervals formed by the tonal degrees—tonic, subdominant, and dominant—are identical in both modes, while the intervals formed with the modal degrees—particularly the mediant, submediant, and leading tone or subtonic—vary. (You will recall from our earlier discussion of minor scales that the supertonic represents somewhat of an anomaly, having both tonal and modal characteristics. The second formed from tonic to supertonic is also identical in these two scales, but for purposes of classification, seconds, having both major and minor quality, must continue to be grouped with thirds, sixths, and sevenths.)

Intervals composed of the tonal degrees are called **perfect** and have only three possible qualities. If we take a perfect interval and make it larger by either raising the upper note or lowering the lower note, the interval becomes directly augmented. Conversely, if we make a perfect interval smaller by lowering the upper note or raising the lower note, the interval becomes directly diminished.

d4    P4    A4        d5    P5    A5        d8    P8    A8        P1    A1

Unisons and octaves are, of course, the same pitch in either the same register or the next register. The augmented unison is the proper name for our by-now-familiar chromatic half step.

Augmented and diminished octaves are found occasionally. The diminished unison seems somewhat of an anomaly but does exist (at least in the minds of music theorists!).

The perfect fourth consists of two whole steps plus a half step, or a major third plus a half step, or a minor third plus a whole step, or simply five half steps. We can calculate the quality of the fourths found in major and minor scales accordingly. Doing so, we will find a preponderance of perfect fourths, with only three important exceptions:

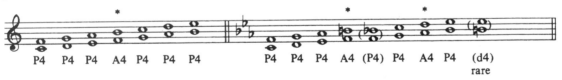

P4  P4  P4  A4  P4  P4  P4        P4  P4  P4  A4  (P4)  P4  A4  P4    (d4)
                                                                      rare

The asterisked fourths are all *augmented*. Since this interval consists of three whole steps, this interval is often termed a **tritone** (abbreviated TT), *tone* here being synonymous with whole step.

W    W    W    = TT

Here are the fifths found in both major and minor scale forms. The perfect fifth is a whole step larger than a perfect fourth, or it can be calculated as a minor third added to a major third.

P5   P5   P5   P5   P5   P5   d5          P5   d5   P5   P5   P5   P5   d5   P5

The diminished fifth (asterisked) is enharmonic to the augmented fourth
and is sometimes also called a tritone (TT).

## Written Exercises

1.  Write perfect fourths *above* the given notes.

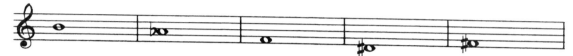

2.  Write perfect fourths *below* the given notes.

3.  Write perfect fifths *above* the given notes.

4.  Write perfect fifths *below* the given notes.

## SIXTHS AND SEVENTHS

We can calculate the qualities of these intervals either by counting half steps or by adding smaller intervals together.

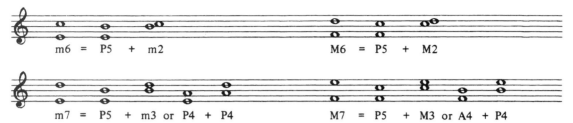

m6  =  P5  +  m2          M6  =  P5  +  M2

m7  =  P5  +  m3 or P4 + P4          M7  =  P5  +  M3 or A4 + P4

Here are sixths and sevenths in their scalar contexts:

M6  M6  m6  M6  M6  m6  m6          m6  m6  M6  M6  m6  M6  M6          M6      m6

Sixths and sevenths, like seconds and thirds, come in four qualities (going from small to large): diminished, minor, major, and augmented.

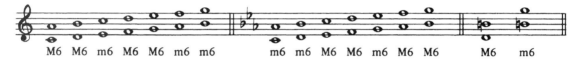

d6          m6          M6          A6          d7          m7          M7          A7 (rare)

## INVERSION OF INTERVALS

Calculating qualities of larger intervals can be cumbersome. There is a shortcut, and it involves turning an interval "upside-down." By this we mean taking *one* of the notes and putting it either up or down an octave.

M3          m6          M3          m6

In our example, a major third has become a minor sixth.

There are two simple rules for determining the size and quality of inverted intervals:

1. The size of the new interval will always be the complement of nine. We can easily summarize this with a simple chart.

   unisons      ⟷      octaves      $(1 + 8 = 9)$
   seconds      ⟷      sevenths     $(2 + 7 = 9)$
   thirds       ⟷      sixths       $(3 + 6 = 9)$
   fourths      ⟷      fifths       $(4 + 5 = 9)$

2. Perfect intervals remain perfect; major intervals become minor (and vice versa); augmented intervals become diminished (and vice versa).

Applying this rule to larger intervals, we first invert the interval and determine the quality of the inverted interval. Then, by applying the rules, we can determine the quality of the original interval.

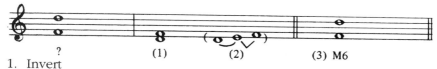

1. Invert
2. Determine quality (whole step plus half step = m3).
3. Apply rules: interval is M6.

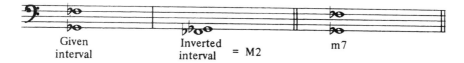

Intervals are typically the most difficult topic encountered in the study of music rudiments. Drill with the computer will make the job easier, since you will soon begin to recognize familiar intervals as they recur in the exercises.

## Computer Exercise

Chapter 9    Intervals
  1. Interval Writing
     Level 2—Major, Minor, & Perfect Intervals Only    Drills #120–121
     Level 3—Sevenths Only    Drills #122–123
  2. Interval Spelling
     Level 2—Major, Minor, & Perfect Intervals Only    Drills #128–129
     Level 3—Sevenths Only    Drills #130–131
  3. Interval Recognition
     Level 2—Major, Minor, & Perfect Intervals Only    Drill #135
     Level 3—Sevenths Only    Drill #136
  4. Inversion of Intervals    Drill #138

## Written Exercises

1.  Invert the given interval. Then identify both intervals as to size and quality.

2.  Analyze these intervals (size and quality) using the standard abbreviations.

3. Analyze the melodic intervals in Examples 1, 3, 6, 7, and 8 in the "Music for Study" section on pages 169, 170, 172, and 173.
4. Construct the indicated intervals *above* the given notes.

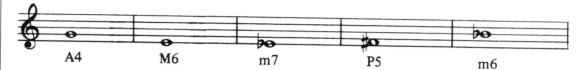

5. Construct the indicated intervals *below* the given notes.

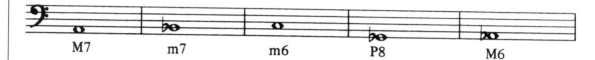

## COMPOUND INTERVALS

None of the intervals we have heretofore discussed have exceeded an octave in size, though it is common for larger intervals to occur. They are called **compound intervals,** and up to a tenth, they are commonly given their proper name:

Those over a tenth are often reduced to simple intervals for ease in identification:

P11   =   P4          P12   =   P5          m13   =   m6

Compound intervals cannot, strictly speaking, be inverted.

## Computer Exercise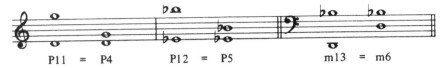

Chapter 9    Intervals
  5.  Compound Interval Recognition    Drill #139

## ALTERATION OF INTERVALS

As we have seen, we can change the quality of any interval by chromatically altering one or both of the notes. We can make the interval larger by *raising* the upper note or *lowering* the lower note.

P4          A4          A4

m3          M3          M3

M6          A6          A6

Conversely, we can make the interval smaller by *lowering* the upper note or *raising* the lower note.

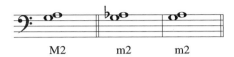

Remember, major intervals first become minor and then diminished. Minor intervals first become major, then augmented.

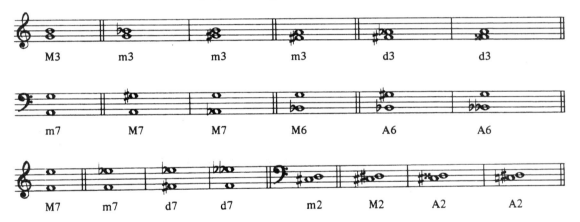

## OTHER PROPERTIES OF INTERVALS

If both notes of an interval are found in a given scale or key, the interval is **diatonic.**

When one of the notes of an interval is foreign to a given scale or key, the interval is **chromatic.** Most augmented and diminished intervals will be chromatic, and it is not unusual for these chromatic intervals to contain both a sharp and a flat.

These are diatonic intervals:

F major:   M3    P5    m6    M2        D minor:   m3    M3    m3    d7

These are chromatic intervals:

F major:   M3    m3    d7        D minor:   m6    d5    A6

Intervals that contain enharmonic notes are naturally called **enharmonic** intervals. Among the more common are the diminished third and the major second, the minor third and the augmented second, the augmented fourth and the diminished fifth, the augmented fifth and the minor sixth, the diminished seventh and the major sixth, and the augmented sixth and the minor seventh. Often, a useful check for the identification of chromatic intervals is to compare them to their enharmonic equivalents.

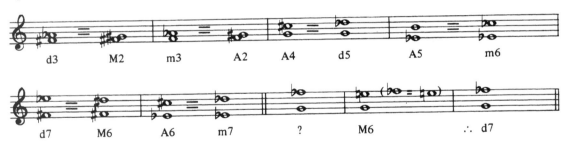

d3        M2        m3        A2    A4        d5        A5        m6

d7        M6        A6        m7        ?        M6        ∴ d7

It is important to note that even though enharmonic intervals sound the same (at least on the piano), they are quite different in the way they are actually used.

Intervals are traditionally categorized as consonant or dissonant. **Consonant intervals** are considered relatively stable, **dissonant intervals** relatively unstable, requiring **resolution** to more consonant intervals. This aspect of intervals is critically dependent on context and changes with style and historical period. With most traditional tonal music, the following categorization can safely be assumed:

*Consonances:* all perfect unisons, fifths, and octaves; all major and minor thirds; all major and minor sixths.

*Dissonances:* all seconds and sevenths and all augmented and diminished intervals.

The perfect fourth may be consonant or dissonant, depending on how it is used.

## Computer Exercise

Chapter 9   Intervals

1.  Interval Writing—Level 4—All Qualities of Simple Intervals
    Drills #124–125
2.  Interval Spelling—Level 4—All Qualities of Simple Intervals
    Drills #132–133
3.  Interval Recognition—Level 4—All Qualities of Simple Intervals
    Drill #137

## Written Exercises

1.  Make the following major intervals *minor,* by altering one of the notes.

2.  Make the following minor intervals *major,* by altering one of the notes.

3.  Make the following intervals *augmented.*

4.  Make the following intervals *diminished.*

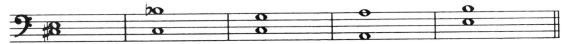

5. Analyze the following intervals, using the standard abbreviations.

## Music for Study

*Simple as it sounds, melodies use just three types of activity: (1) repetition of pitches; (2) stepwise (scalar) or conjunct motion; and (3) skips or disjunct motion. Most melodies strive for a balance of the three, with perhaps a slight preference for conjunct motion. Too much of any one type—but particularly repetition or skips—leads to dull and uninteresting melodies.*

*Listen to and then analyze the following melodies. Where do skips occur? Analyze those intervals. Are the skips large or small? What kind of melodic activity occurs prior to and following skips, particularly large skips?*

**EXAMPLE 1**

*"America, the Beautiful"*    SAMUEL A. WARD (1849–1903)

**EXAMPLE 2**

*Piano Concerto in B♭ Minor, First Movement*

PETER TCHAIKOVSKY (1840–1893)

**EXAMPLE 3**

*"This Can't Be Love"*

RICHARD RODGERS (1902–1979)    LYRICS BY LORENZ HART (1895–1943)

**EXAMPLE 4**

*"Try to Remember"*    HARVEY SCHMIDT (1929– )    LYRICS BY TOM JONES (1928– )

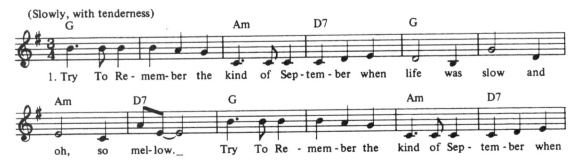

*Example 4 continued*

grass was green and grain was yel-low.__ Try To Re - mem-ber the

kind of Sep - tem - ber when you were a ten - der and cal - low

fel - low.__ Try To Re - mem - ber and if you re - mem - ber, then

fol - low.__

## EXAMPLE 5

*"Edelweiss"*

RICHARD RODGERS (1902–1979)    LYRICS BY OSCAR HAMMERSTEIN II (1895–1960)

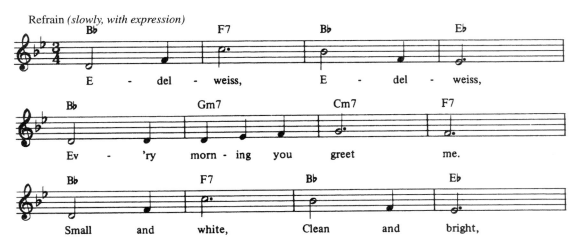

E - del - weiss,    E - del - weiss,

Ev - 'ry morn - ing you greet me.

Small and white, Clean and bright,

*Example 5 continued*

You      look     hap - py     to      meet              me.

**EXAMPLE 6**

*Gavotte*    JOHANN SEBASTIAN BACH (1685–1750)

Consecutive leaps in the same direction generally outline triads, as in this example by Bach. You may wish to return to this example when you have studied Chapter 10.

The result of numerous large skips is often a **compound line.** In Example 7, a single disjunct line seems to form two conjunct lines when certain pitches are registrally related.

**EXAMPLE 7**

*Theme from* Love Story    FRANCIS LAI (1932– )

Here are the two lines that are implied:

Here is another example of a compound line:

**EXAMPLE 8**

*"The Blue Room"*    RICHARD RODGERS (1902–1979)

# TEN

# Chords and Harmony

We have seen that if you play notes in succession you produce a series of melodic intervals, which form a melodic line. Similarly, if you play two notes simultaneously, you sound a harmonic interval. Three or more different pitches played simultaneously results in a **chord.** The following are all chords:

Most music consists of both a linear/horizontal (or melodic) dimension and a vertical (or harmonic) dimension. We typically think of an accompaniment, for example, as consisting of the chords that go along with the tune. But though these chords may be in the background, so to speak, the harmonic dimension is of crucial importance for helping to define the key and structure of the music.

For ease of discussion, we tend to talk about melody and harmony as if they were neat, separate phenomena, which they are not. Most melody tends toward clear harmonic implications, and any series of chords can, in fact, be shown to be a number of melodic lines occurring simultaneously. So in the discussion that follows, remember that a certain amount of overlapping is not only unavoidable but perhaps also desirable.

# TRIADS

The chord structures most common to traditional tonal music are built out of thirds (and are so termed **tertian**). If we put two thirds together like this,

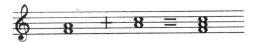

we have a **triad.** Triads, like intervals, have different qualities, and the quality of a triad is determined by the qualities of all the intervals contained in the triad. We name a triad according to its **root,** which is the note on which it is built, and its quality.

The other notes of the triad are named for the intervals they form with the root, namely, the **third** and the **fifth.** We can now describe the four possible qualities of triads:

1. **Major:** M3 from root to third, m3 from third to fifth, and P5 from root to fifth. Major triads are indicated in chord symbols by a capital letter.

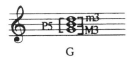

2. **Minor:** m3 from root to third, M3 from third to fifth, and P5 from root to fifth. Minor triads are indicated by a capital letter and a lowercase m.

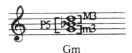

3. **Diminished:** m3 from root to third, m3 from third to fifth, and d5 from root to fifth. Indicated by a capital letter followed by a degree sign, or by the abbreviation dim.

4. **Augmented:** M3 from root to third, M3 from third to fifth, and A5 from root to fifth. Indicated by a capital letter and a plus sign.

G+

Of the four types, major and minor are found most frequently, diminished less frequently, and augmented the least.

You can familiarize yourself with the sounds of each of the four qualities of triads by going to the instruction page for drills #140–142. The computer will highlight each note of the triad as it plays it.

# Computer Exercise

Chapter 10    Chords and Harmony
1. Triad Writing—All Levels    Drills #140–142
2. Triad Spelling—All Levels    Drills #143–145
3. Triad Recognition—All Levels    Drills #146–148

# Written Exercises

1. Write out the indicated triads on the treble staff, using accidentals only (no key signatures). Example:

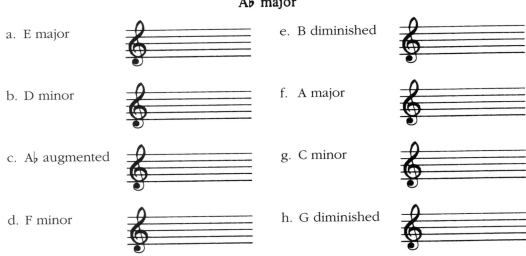

A♭ major

a. E major

b. D minor

c. A♭ augmented

d. F minor

e. B diminished

f. A major

g. C minor

h. G diminished

i.  D♭ major

j.  D augmented

2. Write out the indicated triads on the bass staff, again using only accidentals.

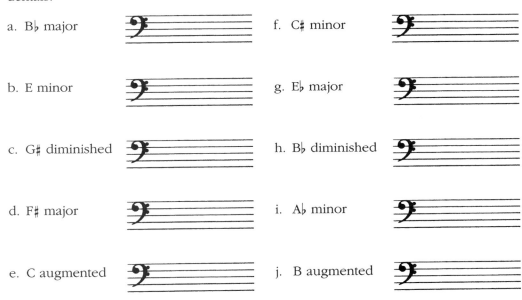

a. B♭ major

b. E minor

c. G♯ diminished

d. F♯ major

e. C augmented

f. C♯ minor

g. E♭ major

h. B♭ diminished

i. A♭ minor

j. B augmented

3. Make the given triads *major* by adding an appropriate accidental to any one of the notes, including the root. No more than one note needs to be altered.

4. Make the given triads *minor*.

5. Make the given triads *augmented*.

6. Make the given triads *diminished*.

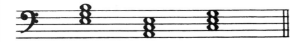

# THE DOMINANT SEVENTH CHORD

If we add another third on top of a triad we have a seventh chord, so named for the interval from the root to the top note. We can build seventh chords on any pitch, and they will have varying qualities, just as triads do. For now, there is one chord of special importance—the dominant seventh. This is a major triad with a minor seventh (indicated by a capital letter followed by the number 7) and is so called because it is the particular chord found built on the dominant in both major and minor.

Remember this chord. You will encounter it frequently.

The computer will demonstrate this chord for you on the instruction page for Drills #149–151. Information on the other qualities of seventh chords will be found in Chapter 13.

## Computer Exercise

Chapter 10    Chords and Harmony

   1. Dominant Seventh Writing    Drill #149
   2. Dominant Seventh Spelling    Drill #150
   3. Dominant Seventh Recognition    Drill #151

## Written Exercises

Write dominant seventh chords on the treble staff, using only accidentals:

1. C7

2. E♭7

3. A7

4. D♭7

5. B7

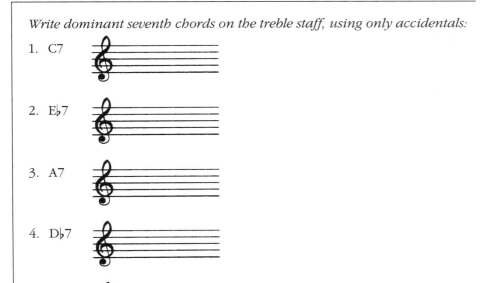

## Music for Study

Triads seldom come as neatly arranged as the examples we have been seeing thus far. Even when the three notes of a triad are arranged together on a single staff, the order of the notes may vary from low to high.

Here is a piano reduction of an excerpt from a Beethoven symphony. Listen to the performance found on your CD-ROM. You will hear predominantly a trio of horns, punctuated by the full orchestra. The horns give us a nice illustration of the possible variety of harmonic and melodic arrangements of triads.

*Symphony No. 3, Third Movement, mm. 167–182*

LUDWIG VAN BEETHOVEN (1770–1827)

*Symphony No. 3, Third Movement, continued*

To determine the identity of the chord, we must rearrange the notes so that
we have a series of thirds. The lowest note will then be the root.

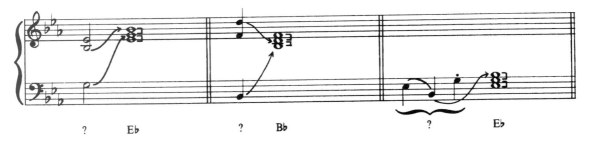

## TEXTURE AND INVERSIONS

One characteristic way of arranging chords is in **four-part harmony.**
You may be familiar with this voicing from hymns and chorales. Because
such pieces are written for four voices, but with predominantly three-note
chords, one note must be duplicated. This is called a **doubling.** Here is a
typical example of four-part harmony:

*"Old Hundredth"*   LOUIS BOURGEOIS (1510–1561)

Praise God from whom all bless - ings flow; Praise Him all crea - tures here be - low; Praise Him a - bove, ye heav'n - ly host; Praise Fa - ther, Son, and Ho - ly Ghost.

In order to identify the chords, we must again reduce the given tones to a series of thirds. This will tell us the root and allow us to determine the quality easily.

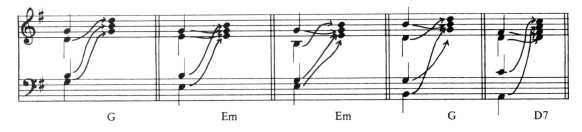

G    Em    Em    G    D7

In four-part harmony, we traditionally designate the various voices with separate stems and name each line according to its range—soprano, alto, tenor, and bass, going from highest to lowest. This is actually vocal-music nomenclature, but the terms are loosely applied to instrumental music as well.

This arrangement of the chords allows us to see how the movement from one chord to another in any one voice actually forms a melodic line. This progression from chord to chord within a given line is called **voice leading** and is a fundamental skill for all composers.

Even with both the melodic and the harmonic dimensions evident here, the balance is probably tipped toward the harmonic in this texture. This is due mostly to the **homorhythmic** character of the music, which means all the voices are moving in basically the same rhythmic values. Lacking any significant rhythmic independence among the lines, the music will be perceived as predominantly a succession of chords, that is, we hear the music *vertically*.

Now, let's look more closely at the lowest voice—the bass line. Much of the time, the bass has the root of the chord. We say that this chord is in **root position.**

But occasionally, the bass will have the *third* of the chord. We say that this chord is in **first inversion.**

(We mustn't, however, confuse this use of the term *inversion* with that associated with intervals. They are related in a way, but the two usages should be kept distinct.) When the bass has the fifth, the chord is said to be in **second inversion.**

Inversions are used to give more melodic interest to the bass line. Important structural chords tend to be in root position, since this is the strongest and most easily identifiable position. Chords in inversion are often indicated in chord symbols like this: C/E bass, G/D bass, and so on.

## Written Exercises

1. Analyze the chords in the following chorale. Indicate with the standard letter symbols the root and quality of each of the chords. Indicate which chords are not in root position.

*"Steal Away"*    SPIRITUAL

2. Return to the example of "Old Hundredth" and identify the position of each of the chords.

There is a seemingly infinite number of ways a composer can arrange a given chord. Some voicings may involve numerous duplications of chord tones in other registers:

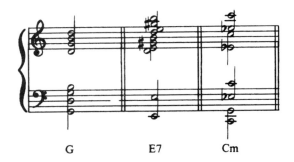

A chord may be broken up, or **arpeggiated,** within a single line:

(Melodic figures that outline chords are called **arpeggios.**)

## Computer Exercise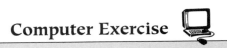

Chapter 10   Chords and Harmony
  7. Chord Recognition   Drills #152–153

## Written Exercises

*Identify the following chords presented in various arrangements. If necessary, reduce to thirds in close spacing, as before.*

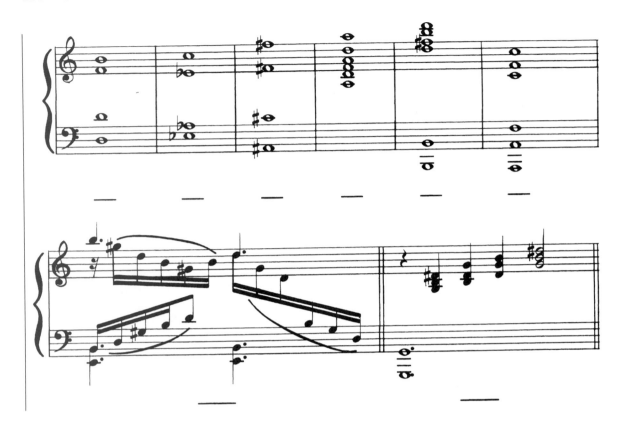

## THE PRIMARY TRIADS

The study of harmony involves both an identification of the chords and some understanding of how and why those chords are used. A detailed study of chord relationships is well beyond the scope of this book, but some basic information can be helpfully applied to the music we routinely encounter, from the classics to the latest pop hit.

Just as certain beats or notes of a scale are more important than others, certain chords within a key have special significance. They are the triads built on tonic, dominant, and subdominant, and they are often called the **primary triads.** We include here the dominant seventh chord, since it occurs even more frequently than the dominant triad. For ease in discussion, chords are often designated by the roman numeral for the scale degree of the root of the chord, as illustrated below. Thus, for a tonic triad (I), we casually say "*one* chord," or for a dominant triad (V) "*five* chord." Major triads are indicated by uppercase roman numerals, minor triads by lowercase, and diminished triads by lowercase roman numerals followed by a degree sign. This system is explained in greater detail in Appendix 2.

For comparison, here are the primary triads in both G major and G minor. Note that the dominant chords in minor derive from the *harmonic* minor scale, with its raised seventh degree, and are accordingly major triad and dominant seventh respectively:

A surprising amount of music can be (and has been) written using only these chords.

The other chords are of lesser significance and are used primarily for variety:

The chords built on the leading tone (marked *) may conveniently be thought of as incomplete dominant sevenths. A major triad is frequently found built on the unaltered seventh scale degree in the minor mode (marked **).

## NONCHORD TONES

We have seen that melodies typically consist of a balance of step and skip. Consecutive skips, or arpeggiations, naturally tend to suggest the underlying chords very clearly. But where the line moves by step, the relationship between the line and the chords becomes more complicated.

Most of the time when there is a solo melodic line with a clearly separate accompaniment, the rhythms of the melody and accompaniment do not coincide, unlike the four-part harmony we saw earlier. The accompaniment may have arpeggios, with a fairly quick value, or offbeat chords.* Whatever the case, the rhythms of the melody will remain largely independent.

Moreover, we can talk about the rate at which chords change, or **harmonic rhythm.** In many styles, even rhythmically active melodies have *slow* harmonic rhythms, meaning few chord changes. A single chord played through several measures is not uncommon. Chords may change every measure, or may change within the measure, but still tend not to follow the rhythms of the melody itself.

For this reason, when a melody is moving by step against a single held chord, certain notes in the melody will obviously not belong to the chord. We call these notes **nonharmonic tones** or **nonchord tones.** We describe them in the manner in which they are approached and left. Here are the most common ones:

1. **Passing tone:** A note that moves from one chord tone to another by step. Several passing tones may occur in direct succession.

2. **Neighboring tone:** A note lying a step or half step above or below a chord tone. The single neighbor is quite common. A double neighbor also occurs frequently and involves a skip from upper to lower neighbor or vice versa. This figure is also known as a **cambiata** or **changing tones.**

---

*For some examples, see below and also in Chapter 12.

Neighbors may also be "freely" introduced. The free neighbor is also sometimes called an **unaccented appoggiatura.**

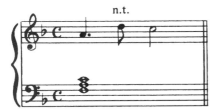

3. **Appoggiatura:** A note introduced by skip and resolved by step, generally in the opposite direction. Roughly translated, it means "leaning tone." This is most typically found on a strong beat.

4. **Suspension:** A strong-beat nonchord tone that is repeated or tied across from a weak beat and resolved down by step.

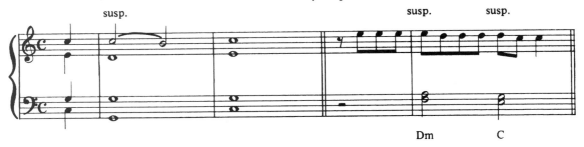

5. **Anticipation:** Literally, a note that anticipates the coming chord tone.

6. **Escape tone:** A tone that moves away by step from the basic direction
of the line and then skips to the expected chord tone.

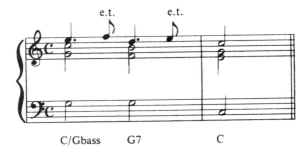

## Exercise

*Here are some melodies with simple accompaniments. Analyze the chords,*
*then pick out and identify all the nonharmonic tones.*

**EXAMPLE 1**

*Scherzo*    FRANZ JOSEF HAYDN (1732–1809)

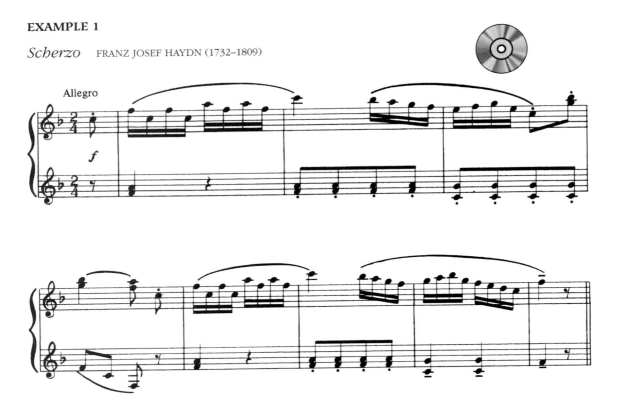

**EXAMPLE 2**

*Waltz in A Major*    FRANZ SCHUBERT (1797–1828)

**EXAMPLE 3**

*"Romanze"*    FELIX MENDELSSOHN (1809–1847)

**EXAMPLE 4**

*"Arabesque"*    JOHANN FRIEDRICH BERGMÜLLER (1806–1874)

**EXAMPLE 5**

*"Romanze"*    LUDWIG VAN BEETHOVEN (1770–1827)

# ELEVEN

# Simple Forms

We come at last to a consideration of musical form. As with almost any piece of art, **form** is that all-embracing term for the devices by which the artist composes, shapes, and organizes the raw material, which in music are the scales, intervals, chords, and rhythms that we have discussed.

Music, to have a convincing form, must have a sense of logical, directed motion from beginning to end. We also expect a certain coherence to the music—the sense that everything belongs. All good music, of whatever genre, seeks a balance between unity and variety, between tension and release, stability and change or flux. Lastly, the music must be clearly articulated; that is, we must know where the "seams" or divisions in the music occur.

## PHRASES AND CADENCES

The basic "building block" of musical form is the **phrase.** A phrase may be defined as a complete musical thought—a gesture having a beginning, a middle, and an end. "Seams" or points of articulation occur at the ends of phrases, so this topic is of considerable importance.

Here are some familiar melodies with chord symbols, as you would find on a lead sheet or sheet music. Where do phrases seem to end? (Where is it logical to take a breath?) What chords are found at those points? What melodic pitches? What is the rhythmic value of the last note of a phrase?

**EXAMPLE 5**

*"Romanze"*    LUDWIG VAN BEETHOVEN (1770–1827)

**EXAMPLE 4**

*"Arabesque"*    JOHANN FRIEDRICH BERGMÜLLER (1806–1874)

**EXAMPLE 2**

*Waltz in A Major*    FRANZ SCHUBERT (1797–1828)

**EXAMPLE 3**

*"Romanze"*    FELIX MENDELSSOHN (1809–1847)

**EXAMPLE 1**

*"'Tis Springtime"*    FRANZ SÜSSMAYER (1766–1803)

**EXAMPLE 2**

*"Softly, Softly"*    CARL MARIA VON WEBER (1786–1826)

**EXAMPLE 3**

*"All Beauty Within You"*    TRADITIONAL ITALIAN

We normally expect to find one of two chords at a **cadence** (the term we apply to a phrase ending). The tonic chord gives us a stronger sense of finality or conclusion because of the inactive scale degrees it contains. Progressions of dominant to tonic at a phrase ending are called **authentic cadences.** Phrase endings on the dominant leave us feeling that the music wants to continue. For this reason, we call a cadence on dominant a **half cadence** or **semi-cadence.** In general terms, an authentic cadence could be characterized as *closed* or *terminal*. The half cadence, by contrast, would be characterized as *open* or *transient*. These are very loose categories. In the case of authentic cadences, a melody ending on tonic will sound more complete than a melody ending on the mediant or dominant. The former is termed a **perfect authentic cadence** (PAC) and the latter an **imperfect authentic cadence** (IAC). The IAC can be considered harmonically closed but at the same time melodically open!

Thinking back to our earlier discussions, we can now see that cadences are the result of the interaction of rhythm, melody, and harmony. We expect cadences to occur on strong beats, and we look for longer note values. Not every progression of dominant to tonic is a cadence, of course. Experience teaches us that phrases tend toward a norm of four measures, and we can always start by looking for cadences every fourth measure.

Two-measure phrases often are found with slow tempos, and three-measure phrases are not uncommon. Eight-measure phrases are likewise found in quick tempos. Irregular-length phrases very likely result from processes of phrase extension or expansion. In this case, the cadence will be very clear!

Points of structural articulation are also a product of the melodic content and design of the phrases. Much of the time, the phrases themselves will contain *motives*. A **motive** is a smaller structural unit, consisting of from one to three beats on average, which has a characteristic and readily recognizable rhythmic and melodic shape, but which does not seem to be complete or free-standing. Rhythmic motives often occur independently; that is, the same rhythmic pattern recurs, but without any systematic pitch conformities. As we have seen, rhythmic figures are crucial for establishing the meter, and as we will see, rhythmic patterning is the most usual method of unifying a series of phrases. Often the motive is germinal and seems to "generate" all the music of the phrase, most commonly through the use of **sequence**—the repetition of the motive at subsequently higher or lower pitch levels. (Look again at Examples 1 and 3 for clear illustrations of motive and sequence.) Motives can also be developed by expanding or contracting intervals within the motive, often keeping one note stationary as a kind of anchor, or by inverting the motive, that is, turning it upside-down. At other times, a phrase may contain two clearly differentiated motivic ideas—one for the opening of the phrase and a second idea for the cadence. (Instances of these devices will be found in the "Examples for the Study of Form" later in the chapter.)

# Music for Study

*The ways melody and harmony interact to establish points of articulation
can be subtle, but they are of vital significance. In the following song, find
the cadence points. Don't forget the text. Are there motives?*

"*The Streets of Laredo*"    TRADITIONAL COWBOY SONG

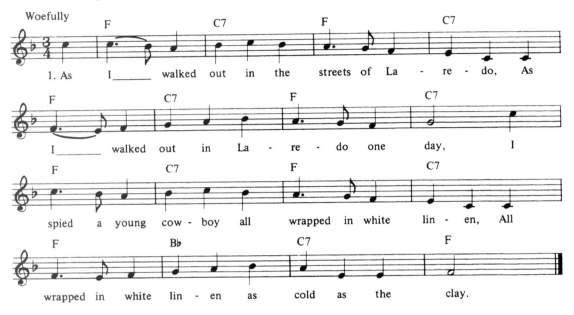

What we observe here, first of all, is that the cadences in measures 4 and 12 are
relatively weaker than those in measures 8 and 16. There is a much greater
degree of continuity of rhythmic motion. The long notes in measures 8 and 16
give a sense of pause in the musical flow. Note the repetition of the rhythmic
motive ♩ ♩ ♩. ♪ ♩. *Now compare the beginnings of the phrases. The motive that
begins the first and third phrase corresponds in both rhythm and pitch. The
same is true of the second and fourth phrases and this establishes a clearly
heard relationship between those phrases. This helps to define the "seam" even
where the cadence is weak, since we understand the repeated music to signal
the beginning of the phrase. Moreover, the first and third phrases also end the
same and the next to last measure of the second phrase repeats the musical
idea of the first (and third) phrase, giving the cadences of the first three phrases
a close affinity. Only the final phrase is significantly different at the cadence.
All this is quite important here, given the repetitious nature of both the rhythm
and the harmony. It is crucial to establish some sort of differentiation, lest we
hear every C7 as implying a cadence, resulting in two-measure phrases.*

# PHRASE RELATIONSHIPS

Look again at the musical examples on pages 195–196. Pay particular attention to the melodic content of the various phrases. Do phrases share melodic material, or are they different? What is the extent of the similarity or dissimilarity?

Form is a product of both cadence and the design or melodic relationships of the various phrases. The first phrase of a piece generally provides us the basis for later references and most often ends with a relatively open cadence, suggesting more music to come.

Very often a first phrase will have the aspect of a question, achieved by a clearly open cadence, usually a half cadence. The following phrase will then provide an answer, achieved by use of a clearly terminal cadence. This question–answer two-phrase structure is called a **period.** The question phrase is called the **antecedent** phrase, and the answer phrase is called the **consequent.**

Many designs are possible. The two phrases may be **parallel**—that is, share the same motives or melodic material. As a rule, only the beginnings of the phrases correspond, with the latter part changed to accommodate the different cadences. There may be slight variations even in the opening parts of the phrases. We can call the phrases parallel even if the material occurs in the second phrase at a different pitch level. (These periods are sometimes called **sequential** periods.)

Alternatively, the two phrases may be **contrasting**—that is, the melodic material may be significantly different.

The design of phrases is indicated by lowercase letters (a, b, c, etc.). Phrases with slight variations are indicated by prime signs along with the letter. For example, a a' indicates a parallel period.

# SONG FORMS

There are two common forms that are typically encountered in songs.

The first possibility is AABA. The initial A phrases may be a repeated phrase or a period. The B phrase is virtually always open, and the last A is a repetition or variation of the *second* A phrase. This is often expanded to 16 or 32 bars. The first 16 may be a repeated 8-bar period, then an 8-bar **bridge** or contrasting section, followed by a return of the first or second period. This is the form of many standard pop songs.

The other possibility is AAB, often called a **bar form.** The B is frequently extended to make it equal in length to both A's together.

# Examples for the Study of Form

*Here are various other musical examples for you to analyze. For each, determine the number of phrases. Where do cadences occur? What devices are used to create the sense of cadence? Identify the type of cadence. Do the phrases form periods? Are there clear motives within the phrases? Are motives sequenced? Are there contrasting motives within the phrase? (Remember that this contrast will not be extreme and that often the different motives will have a fairly uniform rhythmic character.) Using the usual letters of the alphabet, indicate the form of each example.*

## EXAMPLE 1

*"Lullaby"*    JOHANNES BRAHMS (1833–1897)

## EXAMPLE 2

*"Wondrous Love"*    TRADITIONAL

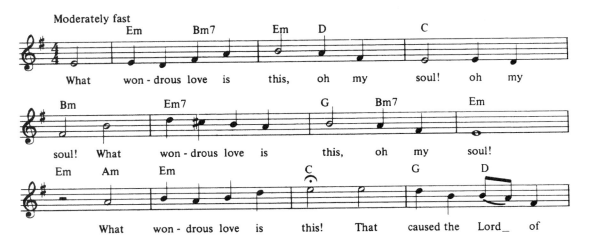

*Example 2 continued*

bliss, To bear the dread - ful curse for my soul, for my

soul, To bear the dread - ful curse for my soul.

## EXAMPLE 3

*"The Ash Grove"* WELSH TUNE

1. Down yon - der green val - ley where stream-lets me- an - der, When twi - light is___ fad-ing I

pen - sive - ly rove, Or at the bright noon-tide in sol - i - tude wan - der A -

mid the dark shades of the lone - ly Ash Grove. 'Twas there while the_ black-bird was

joy - ful- ly_ sing - ing, I first met my_ dear one, the joy of my heart; A -

round us for glad-ness the blue - bells were ring - ing. Ah! then lit - tle___

thought I how soon we should part.

**EXAMPLE 4**

*"Susy, Little Susy"*    FOLKSONG

**EXAMPLE 5**

*Clarinet Quartet, Fourth Movement*    WOLFGANG AMADEUS MOZART (1756–1791)

*Example 5 continued*

### EXAMPLE 6

*"Morning Song"*    CORNELIUS GURLITT (1820–1901)

*Example 6 continued*

**EXAMPLE 7**

*Minuet in F*    FRANZ JOSEF HAYDN (1732–1809)

*Example 7 continued*

## HARMONIZING MELODIES

It follows from what we have said that when harmonizing a given melody, we don't need to supply a chord for every note. We start by using the fewest chords and then add additional chords for the sake of variety or added interest. The most important points to establish chords are at the beginnings and ends of phrases. Here are some examples for study and analysis:

*"Believe Me, If All Those Endearing Young Charms"*
TRADITIONAL

Be - lieve me, if all those en - dear - ing young charms, Which I gaze on so fond - ly to -

day,_____ Were to change by to - mor - row, and fleet in my arms, Like_

fair - y gifts fad - ing a - way,_____ Thou wouldst still be a - dored, as this

mo - ment thou art, Let thy love - li - ness fade as it will,_____ And a -

round the dear ru - in, each wish of my heart, Would en - twine it - self ver - dant - ly still.___

*"Home on the Range"*  TRADITIONAL AMERICAN

## Creative Exercises

1. Complete the following phrases with the indicated cadences:
   a. End with a PAC.

   b. End with an IAC.

   c. End with an open cadence (half cadence or other).

2. Compose answering phrases to the following antecedents, as indicated:
   a. Compose a parallel answer.

b. Compose an answer using the same motive, but at a different pitch level.

c. Compose a contrasting answer.

3. Write original simple song forms, having the indicated designs:
   a. A B A B′(C)
   b. A A′ B A′
   c. A A′ B(B′)

# Melodic Composition at the Computer

*Drill #154 gives you the opportunity to practice completing phrases. The computer will give you the first two measures of a four-measure phrase and a limited palette of note values with which to complete the phrase. You might want to first review the rhythmic composition drills from Chapters 3 and 5. You may end your phrases with either authentic or half cadences. Your instructor may ask you to print out some of your solutions for evaluation.*

# Twelve

# Looking at Music

While looking at a piece of music is indispensable for study, it can obviously (and thankfully) never replace *listening* to the music. Still, as we noted at the beginning of this book, the written score is a very necessary link between the composer and the performer, and all musicians at some point must come to terms with the various skills of music reading. Let's summarize all that we've learned so far.

## WHAT TO LOOK FOR IN A SCORE

1. *Format*. Is there a single staff, grand staff, or several staves grouped into systems?

2. *Basic information*. First, look at the *clef*, then the *key signature,* then the *meter signature*. Remember that the key signature may stand for either a major or a minor key.

   Next, look at the *tempo designation*. This will appear directly above the beginning of the first staff or system. The terms used here are often in Italian and were originally used to specify the character of the music.

   Unless stipulated by a metronome marking, tempo is an *interpretive* decision and is based on both the tempo designation and the meter and average note values.

   Other terms tell us about the character of the music, and here again, these terms are likely to be Italian. Among the most common are these:

*appassionato*—passionately, with great emotion
*espressivo*—expressively, with great feeling
*maestoso*—majestically
*scherzando*—playfully

These terms obviously indicate a certain manner or style of performance and, like tempo terms, give the performer information that can't be communicated by the notes themselves. (Additional terms are defined in the Glossary.)

3. *"Road signs."* A double bar (‖) indicates a major structural division. This particular type of double bar (𝄂) is placed at the end of a composition.

   ‖: :‖ This sign means to repeat all the music within the double bars. Often different endings will be used and are designated like this:

   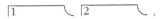

   𝄎. means repeat the previous measure.

   <sup>2</sup>𝄎. means repeat the previous two measures.

   / or // means to repeat the previous figure, generally a beat in duration.

   Here are other directions you will need to know:

   *Da Capo.* (D.C.) Go back to the beginning. (*Capo* is Italian for "head.")
   *Dal Segno.* (D.S.) Go back to the sign (𝄋).
   *al Coda.* (⊕) Jump to the coda, indicated by the (⊕) sign. The term **coda** is derived from the Latin *cauda,* which literally translates as "tail." It refers to a passage that closes a piece of music. While a coda often functions simply as a third or final ending for a song form, in symphonic movements codas may be quite extended.
   *al Fine.* Play to the end or the point indicated by the word *Fine* (Italian for ending).

4. *Texture.* Most music has a principal melody—either an isolated solo line or the top voice of a chordal texture. Occasionally, a melodic line will be found in the bass or in an inner voice. The melody itself will likely tell us the key and may give us important clues as to the phrase structure. The melody will contain important motives and will establish the design of the music through the use of repetition, contrast, or recurrence.

   Harmonies are generally established by inner voices along with the bass. The harmonic progression confirms the key and the phrase structure. Sheet music for popular songs usually contains chord symbols above the vocal line, as a convenience for such instruments as the guitar.

Very often, jazz musicians play from **lead sheets,** which give just the melodic line with the chord symbols. In this case, the written music serves only as a common basis for group improvisation.

5. *Form, shape, and design.* Once the key is established and the phrases have been located, we can think more broadly about the overall shape of the piece. Most music of even small dimension has the sense of moving to some climactic point and then winding down to the ending. This climax may be the highest point of the melodic line, the loudest point, the most intense or dissonant chord structure, or a combination of all of these.

Understanding the devices whereby the composer controls the flow of the music—now increasing, now relaxing the tension—is the ultimate goal of the study of music. We begin by *listening*—and by an initial awareness of our *reactions* to the music. Does it leave us exhilarated, or pensive, or sad, or joyful? Does it make us want to dance, or suggest sober reflection?

Then we *look* at the music itself. What has caused our reaction? Is it the tempo, or the mode, or the character of the melody and/or the chord progressions? Likely it is some of all of these.

The study of music seeks to expand our awareness and thus appreciation of the complexities that go into a work of art. It may also open up new worlds for us, both as listeners and as performers, even if just amateur performances.

Music—as with the other arts—is an act of sharing, or communion, both with our fellow performers and between performer and audience, and ultimately between composer and listener. Through the remarkable language of music notation, we can share the thoughts of Bach or Beethoven or Lennon and McCartney—certainly the richest of heritages!

## Computer Exercise

Chapter 12   Looking at Music
  2. Musical Terms—Tempo Indications   Drill #156
  3. Musical Terms—Character/Expression Indications   Drill #157

# Exercises for Practice in Reading Music

*I. Kuhlau, Opus 55, No. 1* (excerpt)

1. Identify the following terms and symbols:

   ***p***
   ***f***
   ***sf***
   ***mf***
   <

   *poco a poco cresc.*
   dim.
   *espressivo*
   *dolce*

2. Explain the meaning of the meter signature.

3. What is the tempo of the piece? (Define the tempo designation.)

4. What is the initial key?

5. The key changes in measure 53 to _____.

6. What scale is used in mm. 25–28 (right hand)?

7. Identify the chords in the following measures by placing the appropriate chord symbols in the music:

   1, 3, 17, 18, 19, 20, 21, 22, 25, 32, 33;
   53, 55, 56

8. In the first 16 measures, where do cadences probably occur? Identify them as to type.

   In bars 53–68, where do cadences occur? Identify them.

   What is the form of mm. 53–68?

9. What happens beginning in bar 37?

10. Is there a significant motive employed in this piece? If so, write it below:

*Sonata, Opus 55, No. 1*   FRIEDRICH KUHLAU (1786–1832)

*Sonata, Opus 55, No. 1, continued*

*Sonata, Opus 55, No. 1, continued*

## II. Beethoven, Minuet in C

1. Analyze the circled chords. What is the chord in mm. 9–12?

2. Circle and identify the nonchord tones in the following measures:
   4, 10, 17, 18, 19, 20, 28, 31.

3. Define the following terms:
   *Moderato*
   *D.C. al Fine*
   *legato*

4. What is the form of bars 17–24?

*Minuet in C*    LUDWIG VAN BEETHOVEN (1770–1827)

*Minuet in C continued*

III. *Scherzo*    FRANZ JOSEF HAYDN (1732–1809)

Discuss the overall form of this piece, considering both cadences and phrase design.

*Scherzo continued*

## IV. *Bach, Minuet in G*

This is an example of a two-voice composition—one voice in the right hand and the other in the left hand.

1. How does Bach keep the two voices separate and independent? How does he keep them equal? Identify the chords in mm. 1–6. How is the identity of these chords established?

2. Where do cadences occur? How are they established?

3. Are the phrases subdivided? Is a significant motive employed?

4. What is the key of mm. 17–24? How is this new key established? What is the relationship of this key to G major?

5. What occurs beginning at measure 33?

6. Classify the meter signature. What is the unit of the beat? What is the most common note value? The next most common?

7. As was common practice in the baroque period (c. 1620–1750), Bach provides no tempo indication. Do the notes themselves suggest a tempo? If so, what would seem a reasonable metronome marking for the quarter note?

Is the pulse of this piece felt at the beat unit, or at the background unit? Depending on the tempo, might the pulse be felt at the level of the single measure? Experiment with the effect of different tempos on your rhythmic perceptions.

*Minuet in G*    JOHANN SEBASTIAN BACH (1685–1750)

*Minuet in G continued*

## V. Lennon and McCartney, "A Hard Day's Night"

Here is a pop standard from the '60s. It was the title song from the Richard Lester movie that featured the Beatles.

1. Identify the following terms and symbols:

⌢

%

⊕

*D.S. al Coda*

1. _____ 2. _____

---

*"A Hard Day's Night"* can be found in the two-CD boxed set from Apple, CDP 797036-2 and CDP 797039-2.

2. Where do the phrases end? Are the phrases subdivided?

3. How are phrase endings established? Are the traditional cadence labels applicable here?

4. Describe the phrase relationships. Which phrases are alike? Which are different? Describe the overall form of the piece. (Don't ignore the *D.S.*) Compare your analysis to the song forms discussed in Chapter 11.

5. What is the key of the piece? What scale or mode is used in measures 1–8?

6. How might you account for the E flat in measures 11 and 12? Describe the resulting chord in the first half of measure 12.

## "A Hard Day's Night"

JOHN LENNON (1940–1980) AND PAUL MCCARTNEY (1942– )

*"A Hard Day's Night"* continued

*"A Hard Day's Night" continued*

*"A Hard Day's Night"* continued

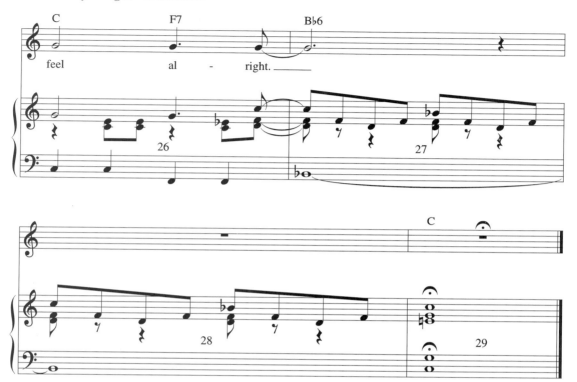

feel     al - right. ____

## VI. *Stuart Balcomb, "¡Ay, Arriba!"*

This is an example of a **lead sheet.** Jazz musicians use these as the basis for improvisation. The jazz repertory, in fact, exists mostly in the form of lead sheets that are collected into so-called "fake books." A jazz combo typically first plays the *head,* which is the tune itself, and then uses the *changes,* or the accompanying harmonies, for *choruses,* which are extended solo improvisations. A chorus may cycle through the changes as often as the performers wish. The "arrangement" may conclude with a final statement of the head, along with its coda, or with an improvised coda. Each player in the group gets a chorus, including members of the rhythm section (usually piano and/or guitar, bass, and drums). The rhythm section plays throughout, supporting the solos of the lead players (trumpet, trombone, saxophones, etc.). This supporting activity is called *comping,* a shortened form of *complementing.* The voicing of chords is left up to the individual players. Pianists and guitar players obviously need to arrange the chords to suit their particular instruments, and for this reason *rhythmic notation* is used for the rhythm section. You can see this illustrated in measures 3–10 in the top staff and in measures 21–24 and measures 33–42 in the lower staff. (Rhythmic notation is also used for the lead players in those sections of improvisation where the composer or arranger wishes to use just the chord symbols.) A samba is a dance of Latin American, probably Brazilian, origins.

1. Identify the following terms and symbols:

𝄋

𝄌

*D.S. al* 𝄌

╱

∕.

2
∕∕.

2. Using measure numbers, chart the sequence the musicians must follow when performing this tune. Don't forget the repeats!

3. Where do phrases end? How are cadences established? Can these cadences be traditionally categorized?

4. Describe the overall form, paying particular attention to the use of similar and contrasting phrases.

*"¡Ay, Arriba!"*    STUART BALCOMB (1951– )

*"¡Ay, Arriba!" continued*

# THIRTEEN

# Topics for Enrichment and Further Study

Throughout the course of our survey of musical fundamentals, we have remarked on the extraordinary variety and diversity of music. With the exception of the music of the Middle Ages (c. 1000–1450), which uses a unique and now obsolete notational system, and some contemporary styles that have developed a number of new, largely graphical, notational devices, all music uses those standard conventions of musical notation that have been the focus of our study. At this point, you should be able to read and understand almost any piece of music. Now you are ready to consider in more detail those topics that may have especially intrigued you.

In this chapter, you will find more on scales, rhythmic devices, and chords. Much of the material on scales and rhythm relates to an area of particular importance and relevance to our own day—that of World Music. This field seeks to enhance our understanding of the music of other cultures and to counter a certain provincialism that would claim a superiority for any particular culture. The chapter also provides additional creative exercises for those of you who wish to explore further the processes of musical composition.

# WORLD MUSIC AND ROOTS MUSIC

The music of particular ethnic groups is often strongly characterized by its scales (along with its rhythms). The music of the Far East, for example, is often pentatonic, while the music of the Balkans region of Eastern Europe has a scalar flavor that often makes us think of Gypsy music. Here are some examples:

## EXAMPLE 1

*"Kimi Gayo"*    NATIONAL ANTHEM OF JAPAN

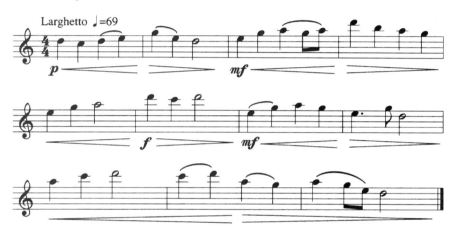

## EXAMPLE 2

*"Sakura" (Cherry Blossoms)*    JAPAN

*Example 2 continued*

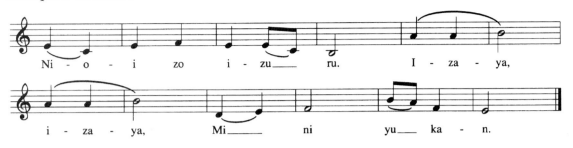

Ni - o - i zo i - zu___ ru.    I - za - ya,

i - za - ya,    Mi___ ni    yu___ ka - n.

Sakura! Sakura! Cherry blossoms floating gently in the sky, as far as the eye can see.
Their fragrance is everywhere. Come, come, let us go see.

**EXAMPLE 3**

*"Liuyue Moli" (Jasmine Flowers of the Sixth Moon)*    TAIWAN

**EXAMPLE 4**

*Romanian Folksong*

**EXAMPLE 5**

*"Karagouna"*    THESSALY

*Example 5 continued*

## EXAMPLE 6

*"I Went Up to Agrafa"*    GREECE

Rhythm, like scales, often gives a unique character to the music of particular cultures. At the same time, it is interesting to observe how the folk music of seemingly diverse cultures has much in common. For example, many cultures have a dance based on simple-duple meter. In the Slavic countries, it's known as a *polka;* in Spanish countries, the *paso doble.* Almost every Western culture also has a relatively quick dance in simple-triple time such as the waltz or the *ländler.*

The music of Africa uses both simple and compound meters, but much of the richness of African drumming derives from the use of compound meters with much syncopation and hemiola. Here is a traditional African song in compound meter:

*"Kyewologo, Kyewologo"*    TRADITIONAL BUGANDAN SONG

*"Kyewologo, Kyewologo" continued*

What scale is being used in this song?

Afro-Cuban music represents a fusion of Hispanic and African rhythmic characteristics and also uses compound meter with frequent syncopations and hemiola.

The folk music of the Balkans region of Eastern Europe often uses a metric structure that we call **irregular** or **mixed meter.** Much of this music was collected by the Hungarian composers Béla Bartók (1881–1945) and Zoltán Kodály (1882–1967). The effect is that of rapidly changing meters, or meters having alternations of simple and compound beats:

This type of rhythm was quickly adapted by twentieth-century composers and becomes a crucial element of contemporary music. Here are two examples of music using this idiom:

*"Dance in Bulgarian Rhythm" from* Mikrokosmos, Vol VI

BÉLA BARTÓK (1881–1945)

*"Blue Rondo a la Turk"*    DAVE BRUBECK (1920– )

"Blue Rondo a la Turk" was first recorded by the original Dave Brubeck Quartet on their ground-breaking LP *Time Out*. This recording has now been reissued as a CD, *Columbia Jazz Masterpieces*, CK #40585.

# SYNTHETIC SCALES

Composers often will invent unusual scales for some specific effect. These often consist of a regular pattern of intervals.

One unique scale is the aptly named **whole-tone scale.** Music using this scale will seem lacking in a secure key center and will either sound restless or have a sense of suspended motion.

*Whole-tone Scale*

**EXAMPLE 1**

*Interlude from* Madama Butterfly    GIACOMO PUCCINI (1858–1924)

The following example uses two scale forms:

A2    (harmonic minor)    A2

Note the symmetrical pattern of steps formed by the variable fourth and sixth scale degrees.

## EXAMPLE 2

*Orientale*    CESAR CUI (1835–1918)

Tradition is sometimes hard to escape. Since Cui was writing in a period where the major–minor system was dominant, he felt compelled perhaps to use the key signature for G minor, even though his scale materials were not traditional. He is thus forced to treat scale degree four as a variable along with six and seven. Might a better solution have been to use only one flat (that for the third scale degree)?

## EXAMPLE 3

*"Fiddler on the Roof"*

JERRY BOCK (1928– )    LYRICS BY SHELDON HARNICK (1924– )

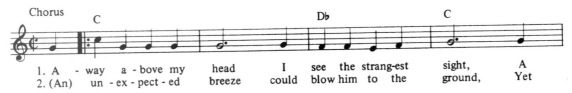

Chorus    C                                          Db              C

1. A - way   a - bove my   head    I   see   the strang-est   sight,    A
2. (An)   un - ex - pect - ed   breeze   could blow him   to   the   ground,   Yet

*Example 3 continued*

## Computer Exercise

Chapter 13   Topics for Enrichment and Further Study
  1. Other Scales   Drill #158

## Exploring Other Scales at the Computer

*Drill #158 gives you the opportunity to listen to the sounds of several of the scales presented in this chapter. Compare the sounds of these scales to those of the major and minor scales.*

## OTHER CHORDS: SEVENTH CHORDS

Seventh chords are found with a number of qualities. The most common one is that of the dominant seventh, which we have defined as a major triad with a minor seventh:

D7

The next most common quality is that of the **minor seventh chord.** This is a minor triad with a minor seventh, and it is indicated by the letter of the root, small m, and the numeral 7. Minor seventh chords are found on supertonic, mediant, and submediant in the major mode; on subdominant and occasionally tonic in the minor mode. The seventh chord built on the dominant of any minor mode (and Mixolydian as well) will be a minor seventh. Use of this quality of the chord is one important contributor to the sound of modal music (that using the modes) as opposed to tonal music (that in either major or minor).

Dm7      Em7      Am7           Fm7      Cm7

A **major seventh chord** is defined as a major triad with a major seventh (indicated with maj7, as in the examples below). Major seventh chords are found on tonic and subdominant in major and on mediant and submediant in minor.

Fmaj7        Cmaj7            A♭maj7       E♭maj7

The **half-diminished seventh chord** is a diminished triad with a minor seventh, and it is indicated by the symbol ø7. This chord is found diatonically only on supertonic in minor and on the leading tone in major.

B<sup>ø</sup>7        D<sup>ø</sup>7

The fully diminished seventh chord—most commonly called simply a **diminished seventh chord**—is a diminished triad with a diminished seventh, and it is symbolized by the degree sign (°). This chord is found diatonically on the raised leading tone in minor but is a very common chord in major as well. (See the following section on borrowed chords.)

F♯°7

## Computer Exercise

Chapter 13    Topics for Enrichment and Further Study
   2. Seventh Chord Recognition—Notice and Listen to the Chords That Are
      *Not* Dominant Sevenths    Drill #159

# OTHER CHORDS: BORROWED CHORDS

We frequently find chords used that are not diatonic to the key. These chords always contain chromatically altered pitches and may conveniently be thought of as borrowed from another key.

Dominant sevenths are routinely found on almost any pitch. They generally resolve or progress to a triad whose root lies a fifth below, and they are analyzable as belonging to the key of that triad. For example, say we

find a D7 in the key of C. This chord will almost always resolve to a G
chord, and we can analyze this chord as the dominant seventh borrowed
from the key of G.

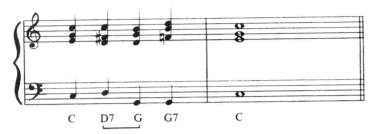

C    D7   G    G7         C

Here are other examples:

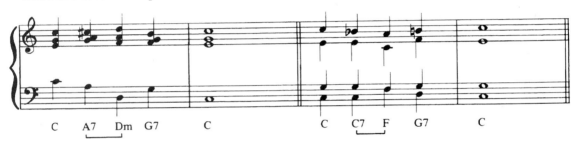

C   A7  Dm  G7        C              C   C7   F   G7        C

Chords are also frequently borrowed from the parallel mode. Common
borrowings from minor to major are the seventh chords on scale degrees
two and seven:

Cmaj : Dø7    B°7

One common device is borrowing a major tonic triad for the final chord
of a piece in minor. This raised third is called, for some unknown reason,
a **piccardy third.**

Cmin :       G7    C

## Exercises

1. Analyze the chords in the indicated measures. Which are diatonic and which are borrowed?

*Minuet, K. 2*    WOLFGANG AMADEUS MOZART (1756–1791)

2. Identify all the chords in this excerpt:

*Symphony No. 4, Third Movement*    JOHANNES BRAHMS (1833–1897)

## OTHER CHORDS: SIXTH CHORDS

One chord frequently encountered in popular music is the triad with an added sixth. This chord is symbolized by the letter-name of the triad plus the numeral 6. The sixth may be added to either major or minor triads, but the sixth itself is virtually always a major sixth. This may require a chromatic alteration.

There is a certain ambiguity about the sixth chord. We can get the same structure by putting a seventh chord in first inversion:

Dm7        Dm7 or F6?        F#°7        F#°7 or Am6?

Even the context will not always allow us to determine exactly which chord is intended. *Style* dictates that the sixth chord is to be expected in contemporary music, particularly pop and jazz, whereas the seventh chord is more likely to be the chord in classical and romantic music.

Both a sixth and a ninth may be found added to triads:

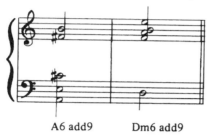

A6 add9        Dm6 add9

A given triad may appear superimposed over a bass note representing the root of another triad. Note the chord symbol.

$\frac{F}{Gbass}$

These chords are frequently encountered with **pedal tones,** which are long, sustained (or repeated) notes, generally in the bass, over which simple progressions occur.

## Exercise

*Write out the chords indicated by the chord symbols on these lead lines of popular songs.*

*Theme from* How the West Was Won    ALFRED NEWMAN (1901–1970)

*Theme from* How the West Was Won *continued*

leath - er;  That's How  The  West  Was  Won._____

*"Over the Rainbow"*    HAROLD ARLEN (1905–1986)

Some - where  o - ver the rain - bow  way  up

high,  There's  a  land that I heard of

*"Over the Rainbow" continued*

once    in    a    lull - a    -    by

# LOOKING AT MUSIC

Béla Bartók was a Hungarian composer who eventually emigrated to the United States. During the early part of the century, he and his countryman Zoltán Kodály were active in researching the folk music of the Balkans. This piano piece, as with so much of Bartók's music, shows the influence of this folk music on his own unique style of composition.

### Bartók, "Evening in the Country"

1. Identify the following terms:

   Lento
   rubato
   *rit.*
   *scherzando*
   Vivo
   non rubato
   Tempo I

2. What is the likely tonal center of this piece? State several reasons for your decision.

3. What scale is used in the first eight measures in the melody? (Disregard the chords here.) Write the scale below and identify it.

4. The first eight measures might also be said to be in what mode? (Consider *both* the melody and the chords!) Write out the scale, using the tonic you determined in question 2.

5. Identify the circled chords, using chord symbols. *Watch the clef signs!*

*"Evening in the Country"*    BÉLA BARTÓK (1881–1945)

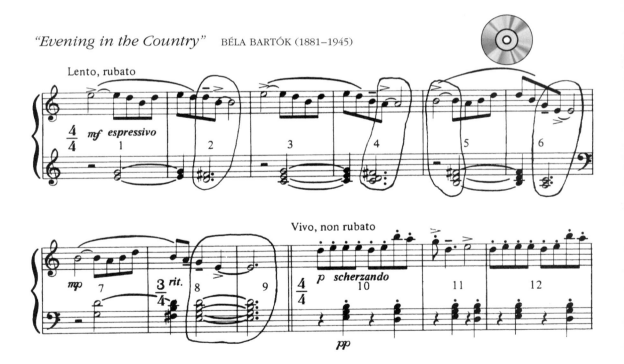

*"Evening in the Country" continued*

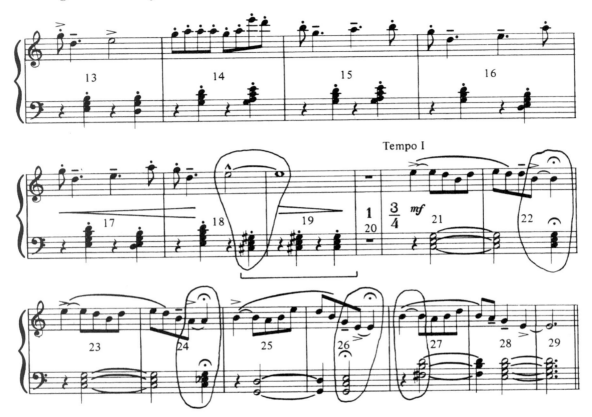

# Creative Exercises

1. *Composing a song.* Review the Creative Exercises from Chapter 11 and the music from Chapter 12. Write a tune, using the AABA design. You may wish to use a poem of from four to eight lines. Look for a poem with reasonably short lines, and let the syllabic stress of the words suggest the meter of the music. When you have completed your melody, you may wish to add a simple accompaniment.

2. *Exploring counterpoint.* As we have seen, contrapuntal music is characterized by a set number of lines which the composer strives to keep both equal and independent. One device for achieving equality is that

of **imitation,** which means the statement of a musical idea in turn in all the voices. A systematic use of imitation creates **canon.** The term *canon* derives from the Latin word for "law" and refers here to the "clue" that tells the performers how a single line of music can be performed so as to create counterpoint. At the least, the "canon" simply indicates by a sign where the subsequent voices begin. However, there is a long tradition in music—going back to the Middle Ages—whereby the directions for performance, or the "canon," are provided in the guise of a riddle.

You are probably familiar with canon through its most popular genre, the **round,** which is in fact a perpetual canon—one written in such a way that it will go on forever or at least until the participants agree to stop. Here is a typical round:

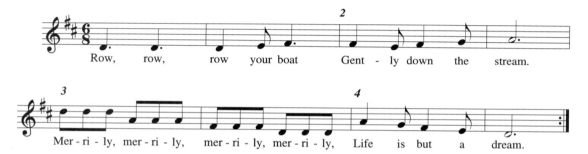

Here is how this round would appear if written out as a four-voice canon:

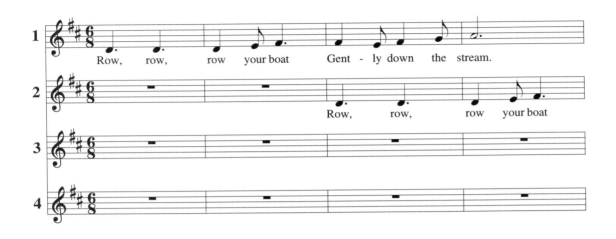

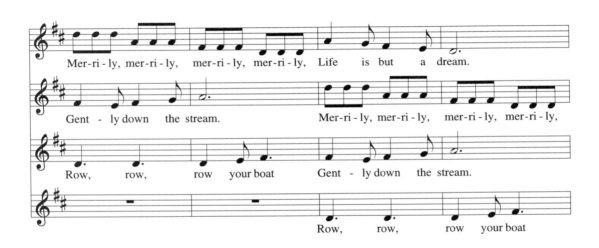

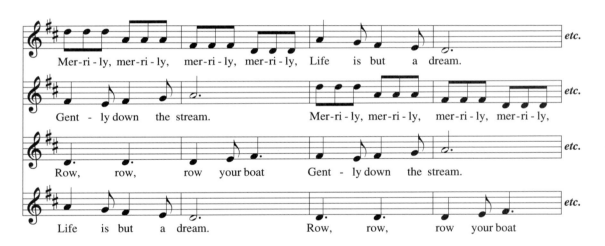

One writes a round in the same way. First write the opening motive:

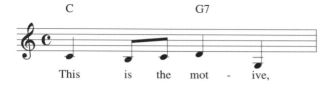

Next, copy this figure to the second voice at its point of entry, and write a counterpoint to the original figure. Note that the harmonic implications of both voices must be the same, but that the counterpoint will probably want to have some rhythmic independence.

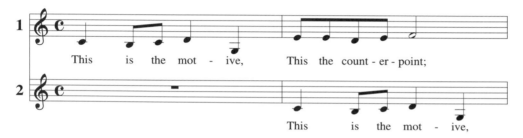

Next, add the third voice and continue working back and forth from voice to voice:

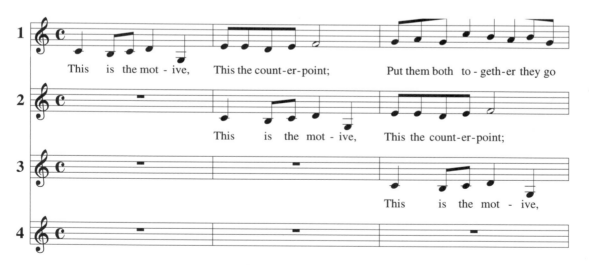

Finally, add a fermata at a point where all the voices may come to a satisfactory close.

Here is the finished canon as it would appear as a single line song:

APPENDIX ONE

# Standard Chord Progressions

Here are several standard chord progressions in simple left-hand voicings for the piano. They may be used for class piano exercises, as the basis for improvisations or composition exercises, or as models for working out simple accompaniments to many of the melodies presented in the body of the book.

Any of these progressions may easily be transposed to other keys and used with other meters.

**NO. 1**

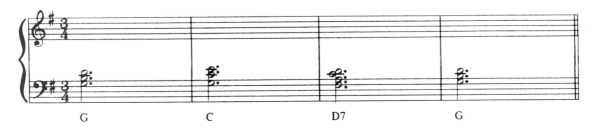

Here is the same progression in the parallel minor mode:

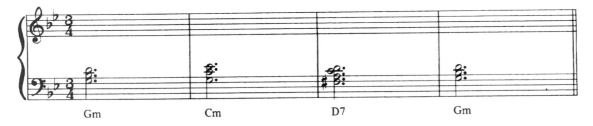

**NO. 2**

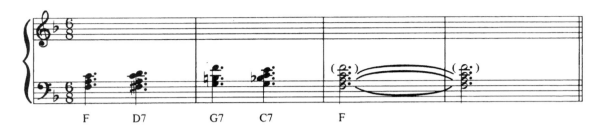

F    D7    G7    C7    F

**NO. 3**

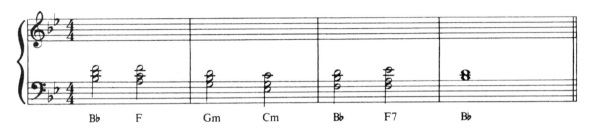

Bb    F    Gm    Cm    Bb    F7    Bb

**NO. 4**

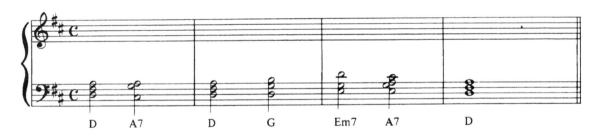

D    A7    D    G    Em7    A7    D

**NO. 5**

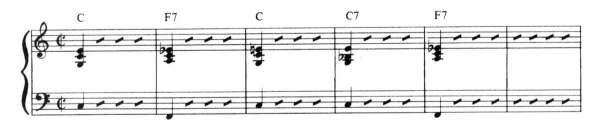

C    F7    C    C7    F7

This is the standard twelve-bar "blues" progression that plays such a prominent part in the history of jazz and popular music. You may want to compose or improvise some typical "walking" bass lines to accompany your tunes. / means to repeat the chord.

# Roman Numeral Chord Designations

In traditional music theory, chords are designated by roman numerals. This system is both descriptive and analytic, in that it deals with both the chords *and* their integral relationships. The system is quite thorough but is somewhat limited in its application outside the realm of "common-practice" music—that music written in a functional, tonal idiom. Most basic theory courses concentrate on the music of the so-called common-practice period (c. 1730–1900), where roman numerals are most relevant. Theory courses dealing with contemporary music (including jazz and popular music) more often use letter designations for chords.

Since many students may want to go on to study traditional theory, here are the basics of the roman numeral system:

1. All chords are designated by the roman numeral corresponding to the scale degree of the root: tonic = I, dominant = V, and so on.
2. Qualities of triads may be designated by using uppercase for major, lowercase for minor, and lowercase with a degree sign for diminished. Here are the diatonic triads in major and minor, along with their roman numeral analyses:

3. Inversions are indicated by using arabic numerals following the roman numeral:

      I6       IV6      I$^6_4$

# Glossary

*accelerando* (accel.)  Getting faster

**accent**  A feeling of stress or weight given to a beat or rhythmic value

**accidental**  A sign placed in front of a note to raise or lower the pitch

**adagio**  A slow tempo, faster than largo, slower than andante

**agitato**  Agitated or excited

**agogic accent**  Accent established by duration

**allegretto**  Moderately fast, somewhat slower than allegro

**allegro**  Quick, lively, bright; a fast tempo

**anacrusis**  An upbeat or pickup, that is, one or more unstressed beats occurring prior to the initial downbeat of a phrase

**andante**  Moderately slow, "walking" tempo

**andantino**  A little faster than andante

**animato**  Animated, with life

**anticipation**  *See* nonharmonic tones

**appassionata**  Passionately

**appoggiatura**  *See* nonharmonic tones

**arpeggio**  The tones of a chord sounded one after the other melodically

**articulations**  Marks used to indicate the relative degree of attack

*a tempo*  In time; used to indicate a return to even time following an *accelerando, ritard,* or *tempo rubato*

**background unit**  That rhythmic value that represents the first or largest division of the beat

**bar**  A unit of division in music equivalent to the total of rhythmic values indicated by the meter signature

**barline**  A thin vertical line separating the music into measures

**bass line**  The lowest sounding voice

**beam**  a thick horizontal line connecting several flagged notes

**beat**  One of a series of regular and ongoing pulses or segments of musical time

*ben*  Well, or marked, as in *ben marcato,* well accented

**bridge**  The contrasting phrase, generally the third, of a simple song form

**cadence**  The ending of a phrase

*calando*  Decreasing in tempo and loudness

**cambiata**  *See* nonharmonic tones

**canon**  A short, single-line piece of music which, when performed by a number of participants entering one after the other, results in counterpoint. The directions for the performance may be given in the form of a riddle or cryptic sentence, and this "canon" or "rule" gives the genre its name. A "perpetual canon"—i.e., one that can go on forever—is called a **round.** Strict imitation in an instrumental or vocal piece is often called "canonic imitation."

*cantabile*  In a singing style, lyrically

**changing tones**  *See* nonharmonic tones

**chorale**  A homophonic texture, most commonly in four voices. In a typical chorale style, all the voice parts move predominantly in the same rhythms, thus creating the effect of a progression of chords. The best known instance of chorale style is the church hymn.

**chord**  Three or more pitches sounded simultaneously

**chromatic**  Referring to notes that do not belong to the basic scale or tonality of the piece

**clef**  A sign used to denominate the lines and spaces of the staff. The treble clef places g1 on the second line, and the bass clef places f on the fourth line. There are also two C clefs: The alto clef places c1 on the third line, and the tenor clef places c1 on the fourth line.

**coda**  The closing portion of a piece of music. A coda may consist of as few as four measures, although codas of large pieces, particularly symphonic movements, may be quite long.

**compound meter**  A meter in which the beat is divided into three equal background units

*con*  With, as in *con moto,* with motion; *con brio,* with fire or vigor; and *con forza,* with force

**consonance**   A feeling of stability, rest, or relaxation in music

**counterpoint**   The art of combining two or more lines into a coherent and musically satisfying texture. *See* polyphony.

**crescendo (cresc.)**   Increasing in volume or loudness

***Da Capo (D.C.)***   Return to the beginning

***Dal Segno (D.S.)***   Go back to the sign 𝄋 and repeat

**diatonic**   Referring to notes that belong to the basic scale or tonality of a piece

**diminuendo (dim.)**   Decreasing in volume

**dissonance**   A feeling of instability or tension in music

***dolce***   Sweetly, gently

***doloroso***   Sadly

**dot**   A sign used to lengthen a note by half; a second dot adds half the value of the first dot

**downbeat**   The first beat of a measure

**duple meter**   A meter having two beats per measure

**duplet**   A sign used to indicate two equal values within a beat of compound meter

**dynamic**   Indication as to volume or loudness (e.g., *piano* and *forte*)

**dynamic accent**   Accent established by volume or attack

***energico***   With energy, vigorously

**enharmonic**   Pitches or intervals that are named differently but are played on the same keys of the piano, for example, F♯ and G♭

**escape tone**   *See* nonharmonic tones

***espressione***   Expression

***espressivo***   Expressively, with great feeling

**fermata (⌢)**   A sign used to indicate a hold or pause on a note or rest; also used occasionally to indicate the ends of phrases in chorales or hymns

***Fine***   The end; *al Fine*—to the end

***forte (f)***   Loud

***fortepiano (fp)***   Loud, then immediately soft

***fortissimo (ff)***   Very loud

**genre**   Type or style of music; often refers to the medium for which the piece is written

***gracioso***   Gracefully

***grave***   Seriously, indicating a slow tempo

**great or grand staff**   A treble and a bass staff braced together and used for most keyboard music

**half cadence**   A cadence that suggests more music to come; an incomplete close, or transient phrase ending

**harmony**   The study of chords and chord relationships; the vertical dimension of music

**hemiola**   Cross accents in simple triple or compound duple meters; the characteristic division of one meter appearing in or alternating with the other

**homophonic**   A texture characterized by an emphasis on the chordal dimension. Two common homophonic textures are chorale texture and melody with accompaniment.

**imitation**   The subsequent restatement of a musical idea in another voice. The interval between the first note of the first voice and the first note of the second voice determines the **interval of imitation.**

**imperfect authentic cadence**   A cadence on tonic harmony, but with a pitch other than tonic in the melody

**interval**   Any two notes considered in their relationship one to another

**irregular meter**   A meter consisting of an odd number of beats (e.g., five or seven) or a combination of simple and compound beats .

**isorhythm**   Regularly recurring patterns of notes that contradict the given meter

**key**   The tonal center of a piece of music as established by the scale and the underlying harmonic progressions

**largo**   Broad, very slow

**lead sheet**   The reduction of a song to just melodic line and chord symbols representing the accompanying harmonies

**ledger lines**   Lines the width of a notehead used to extend the staff both above and below

**legato**   Connected notes played in an unbroken line

***leggiero***   Lightly and delicately

**lento** A slow tempo

*l'istesso tempo* The same tempo

*maestoso* Majestically

*marcato* Marked, with strong accents

*marziale* In a march style

**measure** *See* bar

**melody** The linear dimension of music; melody consists of the movement from pitch to pitch within a line. Most melodies show a balance of movement by skip and by step, with occasional repeated pitches. Melodies are also characterized by their shape or contour (the rise and fall of the line), and their use of rhythmic/motivic patterning.

*meno* Less; with a dynamic mark, it means softer; *meno mosso,* slower, with less motion

**meter** The organization of beats into recurring patterns of accent

**meter signature** Numbers placed at the beginning of the music to indicate the number and value of beat and/or background unit

*mezzo* Medium, as in *mezzo forte* (*mf*), moderately loud; *mezzo piano* (*mp*), moderately soft

**middle C** c1; that C notated "midway" between the treble and bass staves of the grand staff

**mixed meter** *See* irregular meter

**mode** The specific pattern of whole steps and half steps in a scale

**moderato** Moderately, a tempo neither fast nor slow

*molto* Much, as in *molto cresc.,* a great increase in volume

*morendo* Dying away, fading

**motive** A brief musical idea having a definite melodic and/or harmonic character

*moto, mosso* Motion

**neighboring tone** *See* nonharmonic tones

*non* Not, as in *non dim.,* no decrease in volume

**nonharmonic (nonchord) tones** Melodic pitches that do not belong to the underlying harmony. Here are the most common:

    **anticipation** A metrically weak note that anticipates the following chord

    **appoggiatura** A metrically strong note introduced by skip and resolved by step in the opposite direction

    **cambiata, changing tone** A metrically weak note introduced by skip and resolved by step, an unaccented appoggiatura; the term also used for a double neighboring tone

    **escape tone** A metrically weak note that is introduced by step and resolved by skip

    **neighboring tone** A note lying a step above or below a chord tone and returning to the same tone, generally metrically weaker than the chord tone

    **passing tone** A tone that moves stepwise from one chord tone to another, generally metrically weak; accented passing tones are common in descending lines with much the same character as appoggiaturas

    **suspension** A metrically strong note that is prepared as a chord tone of the previous chord and subsequently resolves stepwise downward

**note** A symbol designating a particular rhythmic value and, when placed on a staff, a particular pitch

*octava* (*8ᵛᵃ*) Indicating notes to be played one octave (eight steps) higher or lower (*octava bassa*)

**passing tone** *See* nonharmonic tones

**pedal tone** A generally long note, most often in the bass, against which harmonic progressions occur

**perfect authentic cadence** A cadence on tonic harmony with the tonic pitch in the melody

**period** A two-phrase structure in which a phrase with an open cadence (the antecedent) is followed by a phrase with a closed cadence (the consequent). The two phrases may be parallel in their melodic content or contrasting.

*pesante* Heavily

**phrase** The basic structural unit of music. A phrase is defined by a clear point of melodic and/or harmonic arrival. *See* cadence.

*pianissimo* (*pp*) Very soft

*piano* (*p*) Soft

**piccardy third** A raised third in a final cadential chord in minor

**pickup** A note (or notes) occurring prior to the initial downbeat of a phrase

**pitch**    The relative highness or lowness of a musical sound, a product of the speed of the vibrations in the sound; indicated by the placement of notes on the staff

*più*    More; *più f,* louder; *più mosso,* faster

**plagal cadence**    A terminal cadence progressing from subdominant to tonic harmony

*poco*    A little; *poco a poco,* gradually

**polyphony**    A texture combining several independent melodic lines simultaneously

**presto**    Very fast

**quadruple meter**    A meter having four beats to the measure

**register**    The relative placement of pitches in the gamut from low to high. A given register consists of the octave from one C to the next.

**rest**    A symbol indicating a specific duration of silence

**rhythm**    The various durations or note values found in a piece of music. Rhythm refers more generally to all aspects of the organization of musical time, including meter.

**riff**    A characteristic jazz motive or figure, often used as a background figure or as the basis of improvisations

*rinforzando*    Reinforced, suddenly stressed

*ritard (rit.)*    A slowing of the tempo

*ritardando*    Gradually slowing

*ritenuto*    A holding back, immediately slower

**round**    *See* canon

**rubato**    A free or flexible tempo

**scale**    The pitches used in a given piece of music, ordered from high to low. Diatonic scales include the major scale, the various minor scales, the modes, and the pentatonic scale. The chromatic scale contains all the pitches commonly used in tonal music.

*scherzando, scherzino*    Capriciously; in a light, playful manner

**score**    The written music

*secco*    Dry, short, and crisp

*semplice*    Simply

*sempre*    Always

**sequence**    The repetition of a musical idea at subsequently higher or lower pitch levels

*sforzando (sf, sfz)*    With force or an explosive accent

**simple meter**    A meter in which the beat is divided into two equal background units

**slur**    A curved line indicating a legato articulation; also used as a phrase mark

*sostenuto*    Sustained

*sotto voce*    In an undertone

*spiritoso*    With spirit or verve

**staccato**    Detached, separate

**staff**    Parallel lines and spaces used in music to indicate pitches; the modern staff consists of five lines (and four spaces)

*stringendo*    Accelerating markedly

*subito*    Suddenly

**suspension**    *See* nonharmonic tones

**syncopation**    The displacement of the normal patterns of metric accent

**system**    A number of staves braced together

**tempo**    The rate, pace, or relative speed of the beat

*tenuto*    Held out full length, or even slightly longer

**texture**    The various elements of music—melody, harmony, bass line, accompaniment, etc.—and their mutual relationships

**tie**    A slightly curved line joining two notes into one longer value

**timbre**    The tone colors found in music

*tranquillo*    Tranquilly, peacefully, restfully

**triple meter**    A meter having three beats per measure

**triplet**    A sign used to indicate three equal values within the beat of a simple meter; also used in any situation where three notes are to be played in the time of two notes

*una corda*    With the soft pedal of the piano

**upbeat**    The beat immediately preceding the initial downbeat; the last beat in a measure; the unaccented beats in a measure

**vivace**    Very lively, fast tempo

*vivo*    Lively

# Indexes

---

*****CS:** chord symbols   **SL:** single line   **A:** accompaniment

***CS:** chord symbols   **SL:** single line   **A:** accompaniment